Hezekiah Lord Hosmer

Bacon and Shakespeare in the Sonnets

Hezekiah Lord Hosmer

Bacon and Shakespeare in the Sonnets

ISBN/EAN: 9783337063139

Printed in Europe, USA, Canada, Australia, Japan

Cover: Foto ©Thomas Meinert / pixelio.de

More available books at **www.hansebooks.com**

BACON AND SHAKESPEARE

IN THE SONNETS.

BY

H. L. HOSMER.

SAN FRANCISCO:
THE BANCROFT COMPANY.
1887.

TO

MY DEAR WIFE.

For "Thou Art All the Better Part of Me."

PREFACE.

THE writer of the "Advertisement of the American Publishers" of the Works of Francis Bacon, as the highest eulogy that could be pronounced upon the merits of the illustrious author, writes:—

"In many respects Bacon resembles his immortal contemporary, Shakespeare. Like Shakespeare, he enjoyed the most splendid reputation for genius and ability in his lifetime; like him, he was comparatively undervalued and neglected for ages after his death; and like him, in the present refined and severely scrutinizing era, he has been tried in the hottest furnace of criticism, and has come forth pure gold, whose weight, solidity, and brilliancy can never hereafter be for a moment doubted. It is said of Shakespeare that his fertile genius exhausted the whole world of nature. As a poet, he has undoubtedly done this; and Lord Bacon, as a philosopher, has done the same."

The similarity in the writings which are given to us as the works of Bacon and Shakespeare has received the notice of critics and scholars of every generation since their first appearance, nearly three centuries ago; but a lady of our own country was the first to intimate that the dramas attributed to Shakespeare were written by Lord Bacon. Much controversy among writers has since occurred, and the investigations incident thereto have involved the question in so much doubt, that the interest in its solution will exhaust all conflicting resources before it will be satisfied. As a practical question it may prove of little benefit to the world to know whether Bacon was or was not the author; but if this form of judgment were applied to all the questions of the day, how many would exceed this one in importance? There is certainly an opportunity here for doing a long-delayed act of justice to the memory of one of the greatest benefactors of our race, or of silencing the doubts and suspicions which are gathering around the venerated name of another. If the evidence should irrefutably destroy the idol we have so long worshipped, would the satisfaction be less complete in acknowledging Bacon than Shakespeare? Shall the sentiment which so long has hallowed the shrine of Shakespeare be protected, and the world remain disabused, or the memory of Bacon be rescued, and truth be established?

I ask for a careful perusal of the interpretation of the Sonnets. Undoubtedly the poem will be found to contain many facts in the lives of both Bacon and Shakespeare that have escaped my notice. If those which I have discovered cannot be refuted, or if the Sonnets themselves are not capable of a more reasonable interpretation, then enough has been told to put the supporters of Shakespeare upon their defense.

The Sonnets were undoubtedly written for the purpose of conveying to future ages the true history of the dramas. The Key, and the seemingly surreptitious publication and inexplicable dedication of them, were ingeniously devised to conceal their meaning from contemporary readers. That they have remained so long, and been subjected to so many variant criticisms without comprehensible interpretation, is chargeable to the fact that every writer accepted them and criticised them as the history of the loves of Shakespeare.

For a further and fuller explanation of the reasons governing their publication, I refer the reader to the interpretations themselves. The most I have aspired to accomplish is to aid in discovering the truth.

H. L. H.

San Francisco, October, 1887.

KEY.

Thou and Thine	Impersonation of	Truth.
Thy and Thee	" "	Thought in the abstract.
Thyself	" "	Thought in delineation.
You and Your	" "	Beauty in the abstract.
Yourself	" "	Beauty in delineation.
I, My, Mine, Me . . .	" "	Bacon in person.
Myself	" "	Bacon as author.
My Love	" "	The dramas.
My Friend	" "	Shakespeare.
My Mistress	" "	Tragedy.

BACON AND SHAKESPEARE

IN THE SONNETS.

All critical writers who recognize Shakespeare as the author of these Sonnets have given them a literal interpretation. Let us suppose that they were written by Lord Bacon with the intention of disclosing, through the various forms of analogy, allegory, metaphor, and symbolism, all the real facts concerning the composition of the works attributed to Shakespeare, the reason for transferring the authorship to him, and the manner in which it was done. This is exactly the information to be derived from this poem: —

Sonnet 1.

From fairest **creatures we desire increase,**
That thereby beauty's **rose might never die,**
But as the riper should **by time** decease,
His tender heir might bear his memory;
But Thou, contracted to Thine own bright **eyes,**
Feed'st Thy light's **flame with self-substantial fuel,**
Making a famine where abundance **lies,**
Thyself Thy foe, **to Thy sweet self too cruel.**
Thou, that art now **the world's fresh ornament,**
And only herald **to the gaudy spring,**

> Within Thine own bud buriest Thy content,
> And, tender churl, mak'st waste in niggarding.
> Pity the world, or else this glutton be,
> To eat the world's due, by the grave and Thee.

In natural reasoning, we incline to subjects that are fair, pleasant, and good, and against such as are painful and bad in themselves. Of all subjects, whether animate or inanimate, nothing is fairer in contemplation than Truth. It unravels mystery, exposes error, disarms falsehood, and enlightens the world. Allegorically, Truth being the "fairest" of all "creatures," we desire increase from him, that "beauty's rose," which is "his tender heir," may never die.

In a passive state, Truth is contracted within itself; its "bright eyes" (powers of observation) are closed to all around; its "light's flame" (its Thought, power of production) is fed upon concealment. The world famishes for want of its abundance. It is a foe to Thought, and to its sweet thoughts (its revealed beauty) it is "too cruel."

Truth, when in process of development, is always "the world's fresh ornament," and always the "only herald" of a spring or youth in its new discoveries.

If it buries itself, — is content to remain inactive, — it is like a churl or miser, who, by denying himself, robs the world of its dues.

The author begins this stanza with an address to "Thou" (Truth), "that art now the world's fresh ornament, and only herald to the gaudy spring."

Truth, at the time this was written, was "fresh," not new to the world. The first great manifestation of the revival of letters, after centuries of slumber, was during the reign of Elizabeth. That was emphatically "the gaudy spring" of philosophy, poetry, and literature. The pioneer among the writers of that age, who advocated Truth as the foundation of happiness and progress, was Lord Bacon. He foresaw that without Truth, the glory of his own day would fade, and the world again lapse into ignorance. Hence originated the leading idea of the first seventeen sonnets. Sidney, Spenser, Raleigh, and a host of play-writers besides, had produced many beautiful essays and poems; but they were merely beautiful, and developing no great truth, could have little or no effect in shaping the taste or judgment of the age. It was for Bacon, philosopher as well as poet, to combine Truth and Beauty in a form so attractive as to render them indestructible.

The closing couplet of the first stanza,—

> "Pity the world, or else this glutton be,
> To eat the world's due, by the *grave* and *Thee*,"

means that the world needed not only such truth as the age itself could produce, but a reproduction, also, of those truths so long buried in the "grave" of the Middle Ages. The writers of antiquity must be invoked to give their investigations and discoveries afresh to the world, that modern writers might be inspired with their love of wisdom and learning, and lead to new triumphs in the development of truth.

In the semblance of a young man whom he wishes to persuade into an early marriage, that he may thereby perpetuate himself in his posterity, the author urges Thou (Truth) to perform some labor for the world of enduring value. These impersonations of Thou as Truth, and Thy as Thought, continued to the close of the poem, are first alternated with "You," the impersonation of "Beauty," in the thirteenth stanza. That and the fourteenth, fifteenth, and sixteenth are addressed to You (Beauty), changing the attributes to suit the office he is expected to perform in conjunction with Thou and Thy. Indeed, so closely is the leading idea of marriage, for the purpose of perpetuity, pursued through the first seventeen Sonnets, that the distinction between Thou, Thy, and You (Truth, Thought, and Beauty) has escaped for centuries the careful observation of the most accomplished critics. The opinion generally entertained is, that the object of the author was to persuade a young nobleman to marry. However the Sonnets, as a whole, might be divided to suit the theories formed of them, this with most writers is deemed the leading object.

Mr. Richard Grant White, in his introduction to the Sonnets, gives the following concise statement of some of the many conjectures of writers concerning their object:—

"Farmer thought, or rather guessed, that they were written to William Hart, the poet's nephew. Tyrwhitt suggested that the line,—

'A man in Hue, all Hewes in his controlling,'

in the twentieth Sonnet, indicates William Hughes, or Hews, as their subject. George Chalmers argued that the recipient of impassioned adulation which pervades so many of them was no other than the virgin Queen Elizabeth herself. Dr. Drake supposed that in W. H. we have the transposed initials of Henry Wriothesly, Earl of Southampton; and lastly, Mr. Bowden brought forward William Herbert, Earl of Pembroke, as the beautiful youth, the dearly loved false friend, whose reluctance to marry, and whose readiness to love lightly the wanton and alluring woman whom the poet loved so deeply, were the occasion of these mysterious and impressive poems.

"Mr. Armitage Brown divides the Sonnets into six poems, and thus designates their subjects:—

"First poem,—Sonnets 1 to 26. To his friend, persuading him to marry.

"Second poem,—Sonnets 27 to 55. To his friend, forgiving him for having robbed him of his mistress.

"Third poem,—Sonnets 56 to 77. To his friend, complaining of his coldness, and warning him of life's decay.

"Fourth poem,—Sonnets 78 to 101. To his friend, complaining that he prefers another poet's praises, and reproving him for faults that may injure his character.

"Fifth poem,—Sonnets 102 to 126. To his

friend, excusing himself for having been some time silent, and disclaiming the charge of inconstancy.

"Sixth poem,—Sonnets 127 to 152. To his mistress, on her infidelity."

Mr. White advances the opinion that "some of them are addressed to a woman, others to a lad, others to a man; in three Shakespeare speaks unmistakably of himself and upon subjects purely personal, and the last two are merely fanciful and independent productions."

It was the opinion of Mr. Dyer that the Sonnets were composed "in an assumed character, on different subjects and at different times."

"Five of the Sonnets, Nos. 80, 83, 85, 86, and 121," Mr. White thinks were "evidently written to be presented to some lady who had verses addressed to her by at least one other person than the supposed writer of these, for the praises of another poet are explicitly mentioned in them." No. 78, in his opinion, was addressed to one "who was the theme of many pens, for it contains these lines:—

"'So oft have I invok'd Thee for my Muse,
And found such fair assistance in my verse,
As every alien pen hath got my use,
And under thee their poesy disperse;

. . . . . .

In others' works thou dost but mend the style,
And arts with thy sweet graces graced be.'"

Not only these lines, but the entire one hundred and fifty-four stanzas, are, as I think, perfectly comprehensible when the Key is used to unfold their meaning. Consider Thee as the impersonation of Thought in the foregoing lines, and we learn simply that the writer has been so successful in the delineation of Truth, that the other writers of the age ("every alien pen") are emulous of similar success, and are adopting Thought as a basis for their poetry,—

"Under Thee their poesy disperse."

In the last two lines he intimates that in this attempt at imitation they only "mend the style" of their composition. It is too artificial to be true to nature, but is nevertheless graced or made better by the attempt,—

"And arts with Thy (Thought's) sweet graces graced be."

All the incongruities, entanglements, and intricacies of the poem, by application of the Key, become consistent, and in proper sequence, from opening to close, with the wonderful history they have so long concealed. The poem is an entire history.

Sonnet 2.

When forty winters shall beseige Thy brow,
And dig deep trenches in Thy beauty's field,
Thy youth's proud livery, so gaz'd on now,
Will be a tatter'd weed, of small worth held;
Then being ask'd where all Thy beauty lies,
Where all the treasure of Thy lusty days,
To say, within Thine own deep-sunken eyes,
Were an all-eating shame and thriftless praise.
How much more praise deserv'd Thy beauty's use,
If Thou couldst answer, "This fair child of mine
Shall sum my count and make my old excuse,"
Proving his beauty by succession Thine!
This were to be new made when Thou art old,
And see Thy blood warm when Thou feel'st it cold.

The meaning sought to be conveyed by the poet in this stanza is, that if he should delay revealing his conception of Truth until he was forty years old, Time would then have destroyed the freshness and exuberance of his thoughts, and impaired his power to delineate beauty as he saw it in early life. The "proud livery" of that dawning period would be faded and worn, with the "deep trenches" of age and care, and the "sunken eye" of a careless life would tell of the "all-eating" effects of neglect and misuse. "Thriftless praise" (barren reward and a useless life) would be the result. If, instead of this, he could show by his work some "fair child of mine" (that he had produced some evidence of his genius), that would "sum his count" (affirm the promises of his youth), "and make my old excuse" (the works would be substituted for the "old excuse" he had habitually given for his negligence), and they would prove also his power of delineation. In these works he would be recreated in his age, and witness the effect of his labors, after his powers were exhausted.

> "Thy youth's proud livery, so gaz'd on now,
> Will be a tatter'd weed, of small worth held."

The "Promus of Lord Bacon," compiled by Mrs. Pott, and published a few years ago, is but one of several commonplace books found among his papers after his decease. It is composed of aphorisms, trite sayings, wise mixims, and parts of passages, selected without any apparent object, from the writings of learned men of antiquity, and of the ages preceding that of Elizabeth. Mrs. Pott has traced the analogy in many instances between these disjointed thoughts and passages from the dramas attributed to Shakespeare, in which they appear in more gorgeous dress; and thus furnished a strong inferential argument in favor of the Baconian theory of authorship.

This "youth's proud livery," which would be a "tatter'd weed" if not used before the age of forty, was the Truth as set forth in these commonplace books, elaborated and embellished by his powers of composition. It would be mere "tatters" if unused.

SONNET 3.

Look in Thy glass, and tell the face Thou viewest
Now is the time that face should form another;
Whose fresh repair, if now Thou not renewest,
Thou dost beguile the world, unbless some mother;
For where is she so fair, whose unear'd womb
Disdains the tillage of Thy husbandry?
Or who is he so fond will be the tomb
Of his self-love, to stop posterity?
Thou art Thy mother's glass, and she in Thee
Calls back the lovely April of her prime;
So Thou through windows of Thine age shalt see,
Despite of wrinkles, this Thy golden time.
　But if Thou live, remember'd not to be,
　Die single, and Thine image dies with Thee.

The Rev. John Lord, in his admirable lecture on Queen Elizabeth, winds up a graphic description of the condition of England at the time of her accession, in the following glowing language:—

"In England, in Elizabeth's time, there was a noble material for Christianity and art and literature to work upon, and to develop a civilization such as had not existed previously on this earth, — a civilization destined to spread throughout the world, in new inventions, laws, language, and literature, binding hostile races together, and proclaiming the sovereignty of intelligence."

"Look in thy glass." "Glass" as used here, and in other places in the poem, means past life. Look in his past life, and "tell the face Thou viewest" (his culture, opportunities, education, and natural abilities) that the time of life has come to him when he should utilize these attainments in the production of some work reflecting their powers and beauties. Failing of this, "thou dost beguile the world" (the world will be deceived in the opinion it has formed of his genius), and "unbless some mother" (some subject suited to his taste will fail of investigation). There are no "unear'd" (original) matters which Thy (Thought) could not examine with profit, and he would be selfish indeed, who, having the power, would keep his thoughts in himself as in a "tomb," and so rob "posterity" of them. As his mother gave her thoughts to the revealment of Truth, so in his thoughts she would see her life reproduced. Truth, despite of age, would be encircled by his youthful thoughts, and he would see that this had proved the time for their improvement. There was work for him to do, and it would be his own fault if he neglected to do it. The age was full of opportunities, and great men were rapidly improving them. A mighty revolution in the world's history was in progress, and if he failed to participate in it, and remained unknown, he would "die single" (be forgotten), and his "image" (his memory) would die with him.

SONNET 4.

Unthrifty loveliness, why dost Thou spend
Upon Thyself Thy beauty's legacy?
Nature's bequest gives nothing, but doth lend,
And being frank, she lends to those are free.
Then, beauteous niggard, why dost Thou abuse
The bounteous largess given Thee to give?
Profitless usurer, why dost Thou use
So great a sum of sums, yet canst not live?
For having traffic with Thyself alone,
Thou of Thyself Thy sweet self dost deceive.
Then how, when nature calls Thee to be gone,
What acceptable audit canst Thou leave?
  Thy unus'd beauty must be tomb'd with Thee,
  Which, used, lives Thy executor to be.

Nature, which gives no more to him than others, has lent him much more, and is entitled to a proper return for it. "Being frank, she lends to those are free" (her kindness, frankly bestowed, should be freely given to the world). Why does he abuse the "bounteous largess given him to give"? (Why should he, so greatly endowed, neglect to make others participators of his gifts?) Why use it, and not live in it? In other words, why let his great powers (his thought and beauty) remain in himself, when so much good can be done by devoting them to some great service that will outlive him, and give him an undying name.

It is wrong not to "live" (perpetuate himself), with "so great a sum of sums" (such wide and varied powers). He belies himself by keeping them unused; and will leave nothing to show that he has ever lived. All his "unus'd beauty" (those talents, both acquired and natural), which, if devoted to proper uses, would give him character and renown, and be to him at death as an "executor," will be "tomb'd with Thee" (buried with his thoughts, and lost to the world).

Sonnet 5.

Those hours, that with gentle work did frame
The lovely gaze where every eye doth dwell,
Will play the tyrants to the very same,
And that unfair which fairly doth excel;
For never-resting time leads summer on
To hideous winter, and confounds him there;
Sap check'd with frost, and lusty leaves quite gone,
Beauty o'ersnow'd, and bareness everywhere:
Then, were not summer's distillation left,
A liquid prisoner pent in walls of glass,
Beauty's effect with beauty were bereft,
Nor it, nor no remembrance what it was:
But flowers distill'd, though they with winter meet,
Leese but their show, their substance still lives sweet.

If he neglects to use his powers, the hours of study, which have made him so accomplished in learning, intelligence, and poetry, will cause him to be scorned and despised for his neglect, when "never-resting time leads summer on to hideous winter" (when his youth is passed, and dreary old age comes). He will then be like a tree whose sap is frozen, bare of leaves; all its beauty covered with snow, and its limbs, and all around it, naked and cold. But if he improves his opportunities, they will be to him like "summer's distillation" (the life-preserving principle) to the tree and to flowers, which no winter with its frost and snow and bareness can rob of their perfume.

SONNET 6.

Then let not winter's ragged hand deface
In Thee Thy summer, ere Thou be distill'd:
Make sweet some vial; treasure Thou some place
With beauty's treasure ere it be self-kill'd.
That use is not forbidden usury,
Which happies those that pay the willing loan;,
That 's for Thyself to breed another Thee,
Or ten times happier, be it ten for one;
Ten times Thyself were happier than Thou art,
If ten of Thine ten times refigur'd Thee:
Then what could death do, if Thou shouldst depart,
Leaving Thee living in posterity?
  Be not self-will'd, for Thou art much too fair
  To be Death's conquest, and make worms Thine heir.

He should protect his age from such disasters, as from neglect await it, by producing something in his youth. His power to delineate Truth and Beauty should be displayed in his thoughts, before it is destroyed by age. There is abundant opportunity for all that he can do; "that use is not forbidden usury" (where the work is well done). He may produce one or "ten," or "ten times ten," and the greater the number, the greater the good, if "they refigure Thee" (if they are born of his thoughts). In such case death cannot destroy him. His thoughts will live in posterity (his works). And as he is "much too fair" (possessed of the requisite qualifications), he should anticipate death by his labors, and win immortality in his works.

SONNET 7.

Lo, in the orient when the gracious light
Lifts up his burning head, each under eye
Doth homage to his new-appearing sight,
Serving with looks his sacred majesty;
And having climb'd the steep-up heavenly hill,
Resembling strong youth in his middle age,
Yet mortal looks adore his beauty still,
Attending on his golden pilgrimage;
But when from highmost pitch, with weary car,
Like feeble age, he reeleth from the day,
The eyes, fore duteous, now converted are
From his low tract, and look another way:
So Thou, Thyself outgoing in Thy noon,
Unlook'd on, diest, unless Thou get a son.

As of the sun, so grand in its rising and ascension to its meridian, like a strong youth in middle life, commanding the "homage" of all, and so "weary" and "feeble" in its decline, "like feeble age," causing all to "look another way," so it may be said of him, that unless he prepares some undying testimonial of his genius before the noon, or middle of his life, no record will remain to perpetuate his name or memory.

SONNET 8.

Music to hear, why **hear'st Thou** music sadly?
Sweets with sweets war not, joy delights in joy.
Why lov'st Thou that which Thou receiv'st not gladly,
Or else receiv'st with pleasure Thine annoy?
If the true concord of well-tuned sounds,
By unions married, do offend thine ear,
They do but sweetly chide Thee, who confounds
In singleness the parts that Thou shouldst bear.
Mark how one string, sweet husband to another,
Strikes **each** in each by mutual ordering,
Resembling sire and child and happy mother,
Who, all in one, one pleasing note do sing;
  Whose speechless song, being many, seeming one,
  Sings this to Thee: "Thou single wilt prove none."

So of music also! **It is** only offensive **to that** ear which confounds its parts (hears them **singly**); but when **all** the strings strike in order, **like "sire and** child **and** happy mother," and all **are heard as** "one pleasing note" **(in** perfect unison), then **the** notes, **being** many, **strike upon** the ear as one, and these "sing **to** him" (enforce our argument). "Thou single wilt prove **none**" (Truth **alone,** without a development, is intangible and **useless).**

SONNET 9.

Is it for fear to wet a widow's eye
That Thou consum'st Thyself in single life?
Ah! if Thou issueless shalt hap to die,
The world will wail Thee like a makeless wife;
The world will be **Thy widow, and still weep**
That Thou no form **of Thee hast left behind,**
When every private widow well may keep,
By children's eyes, her husband's shape in mind.

Look, what an unthrift in the world doth spend
Shifts but his place, for still the world enjoys it;
But beauty's waste hath in the world an end,
And kept unus'd, the user so destroys it.
No love toward others in that bosom sits,
That on himself such murtherous shame commits.

Is it for fear of failure to exhibit Truth correctly that he remains silent? If he fails to produce a work worthy of himself, "the world will wail him like a makeless wife." (As a wife who sorrowed that she had never been blessed with children, so the world will regret that one so gifted should die without leaving any record of his abilities; and in that sense will be his widow, and remember him only as one who wasted his powers, leaving nothing to tell that he had ever existed.) He was an "unthrift" (a worthless fellow), who had Beauty in possession, but never used it, or delineated it, and it was necessarily of no account. He could have no love or regard for his fellows, as was evident from the "murtherous shame" (the neglect and sacrifice) of his own powers.

Sonnet 10.

For shame! deny that Thou bear'st love to any,
Who for Thyself art so unprovident.
Grant, if Thou wilt, Thou art belov'd of many,
But that Thou none lov'st is most evident;
For Thou art so possess'd with murtherous hate,
That 'gainst Thyself Thou stick'st not to conspire,
Seeking that beauteous roof to ruinate,
Which to repair should be Thy chief desire.

O, change Thy thought, that I may change My mind!
Shall hate be fairer lodg'd than gentle love?
Be, as Thy presence is, gracious and kind,
Or to Thyself at least kind-hearted prove;
Make Thee another self, for love of Me,
That beauty still may live in Thine or Thee.

In this stanza he rebukes Thou (Truth), charging him with indifference to all, and entire disregard of his own powers. He cares nothing for the esteem in which others hold him, but is so neglectful of his own thoughts, that all his acquirements, which should be devoted to some good purpose, will fall into decay from disuse. "O, change Thy thought, that I may change My mind," is the same as if he had besought Truth to aid him in giving direction to his thoughts. Such "hate" (indifference) as Truth exhibits, and such "love" (desire) as he feels to work, ought not to dwell in the same person. He contemplates his thoughts with pleasure, and asks for their kindness in return, and "for love of Me make Thee another self" (with Truth as the foundation, he will produce some work worthy of himself). "That Beauty still may live in Thine and Thee" (which shall display the imagery and brilliancy of his own thoughts, and give them endurance).

SONNET 11.

As fast as Thou shalt wane, so fast Thou growest
In one of Thine, from that which Thou departest;
And that fresh blood which youngly Thou bestowest,
Thou may'st call Thine, when Thou from youth convertest.

Herein lives wisdom, beauty, and increase;
Without this, folly, age, and cold decay:
If all were minded so, the time should cease,
And threescore year would make the world away.
Let those whom Nature hath not made for store,
Harsh, featureless, and rude, barrenly perish:
Look, whom she best endow'd, she gave the more,
Which bounteous gift Thou shouldst in bounty cherish.
She carv'd Thee for her seal, and meant thereby
Thou shouldst print more, not let that copy die.

In the promise here made to Thou (Truth), that "as fast as Thou shalt wane, so fast Thou growest in one of Thine," we are assured that as soon as one drama is completed another will be begun, in which Truth will be exhibited in his thought, and that "fresh blood, which youngly thou bestowest" (these early productions of his genius), "Thou may'st call Thine when Thou from youth convertest" (will bear testimony to his great powers of delineation when he is old). All that is good and beautiful in his nature will assist him in his labors, but if he neglects them all, his worst qualities will take possession of him, and he will be forgotten. If such a course of life were pursued by all, the world would be destitute of truth in "threescore year" (a single life). In the remaining lines of this stanza he shows that he had a full appreciation of his own great abilities, as contrasted with the common allotment. He owed it to Nature, which had so grandly endowed him, to make a corresponding return. She had given him more than those whom "she best endowed."

She had, indeed, "carv'd Thee (Thought) for her seal," meaning thereby that Truth should multiply himself, and never die.

SONNET 12.

When I do count the clock that tells the time,
And see the brave day sunk in hideous night;
When I behold the violet past prime,
And sable curls, all silver'd o'er with white;
When lofty trees I see barren of leaves,
Which erst from heat did canopy the herd,
And summer's green, all girded up in sheaves,
Borne on the bier with white and bristly beard:
Then of Thy beauty do I question make,
That Thou among the wastes of time must go,
Since sweets and beauties do themselves forsake,
And die as fast as they see others grow.
And nothing 'gainst Time's scythe can make defence,
Save breed, to brave him when he takes Thee hence.

As the day obscured by night; as the violet when fading to decay; as the sable hair when silvered; as tall trees bereft of foliage; as the green summer fields, gathered into bristly and bearded crops,—so, since it thus appears that natural objects are forsaken by the appendages that give them beauty and sweetness, will it be with the beauty and sweetness of his thoughts, and they will by time be wasted, unless he perpetuates himself by "breed" (the production of works worthy of himself). Therein is his only defence against Time.

The next stanza is addressed to Beauty (impersonated as You). Those preceding have been addressed to Truth (impersonated as Thou) and Thy (impersonated as Thought). Thou, Thy, and You are represented as young men. Thou as the active, vigorous worker. The solid, reliable work of the dramas (all that gives them permanent value) is to be furnished by Thou, and this store is to be wrought into form by Thy (Thought). Beauty is to furnish ornament, imagery, creative power, and every conceivable grace that will render Truth attractive without impairing his might or perverting the ends he has in view.

It has been suggested by some writers who favor the Baconian theory that the dramas were intended, when written, to form the fourth part of the Novum Organum. They were designed to illustrate life in character upon a philosophical basis, and not for theatrical representation. However this may have been, and how well soever they might have accomplished such a purpose, with nothing but conjecture for this opinion, we can consider them only in their isolated condition. The great merit of the dramas consists in the union of Truth and Beauty as everywhere exhibited in them. It is the one profound thought appearing in them which has given them their vast superiority over the works of all other writers. There is hardly a thought or character in the whole range that could be removed without affecting the grand entirety of the work in which it appears. As problems in the philosophy of mind, aside from their attractive garb of language and imagery, they will always rank with the philosophical works of the best writers. It has been truly said by Charles Lamb and others that they exceed the powers of the mimic art properly to display them; at the same time, it is also true that it will be a sad event for the theatre, when it abandons them, to give place to the wretched representations of this generation.

Sonnet 13.

O, that You **were** Yourself! but, **love, You are**
No longer Yours, than You **Yourself here live;**
Against this coming end You should prepare,
And Your sweet semblance to some other give.
So should **that beauty which** You hold in lease
Find no determination; then You were
Yourself again after Yourself's decease,
When **Your** sweet issue Your sweet **form should bear.**
Who lets so fair **a** house fall to decay,
Which husbandry in honor might uphold,
Against the stormy gusts of winter's day
And barren rage of death's eternal cold?
  O, none but unthrifts! dear, my love, You know
  You **had** a father; let Your son say so.

You (Beauty), as Thou (Truth), in the preceding stanza, is urged to be himself, but he can only be himself while he lives, and he can live only in the object which he adorns. He is both evanescent, in that he fades with a thought, and dependent, because he has no separate life. This ethereality he is warned to overcome, by giving his "sweet semblance" (his varied powers of creation, fancy, grace, sublimity, dignity) to another, in whom it may be perpetuated. His gift should "find no determination" (it should be entire, unlimited). This will make You (Beauty) "Yourself again after Yourself's decease" (he will renew his life in every work that he adorns). When such a gift, so rich in attributes, can be honorably saved from "the stormy gusts of winter's day" (old age and its infirmities), and "barren rage of death's eternal cold" (negligence and disuse), who but an "unthrift" (a worthless fellow) will not avail himself of the means to develop it? As You (Beauty) depended upon a father (some object) for your life, so by a "son" (like dependence) must yours continue.

SONNET 14.

Nor from the stars do I my judgment pluck;
And yet methinks I have astronomy,
But not to tell of good or evil luck,
Of plagues, of dearths, or seasons' quality;
Nor can I fortune to brief minutes tell,
Pointing to each his thunder, rain, and wind,
Or say with princes if it shall go well,
By oft predict that I in heaven find:
But from Thine eyes my knowledge I derive,
And, constant stars, in them I read such art
As Truth and Beauty shall together thrive,
If from Thyself to store Thou wouldst convert;
Or else of Thee this I prognosticate, —
Thy end is Truth's and Beauty's doom and date.

The poet, though familiar with astronomy, has not consulted the stars, nor does his knowledge of them enable him to foretell their influence upon the fortune of any one, or upon the varied evils which befall the world. He does not understand their effect well enough to determine the time when fortune will come, nor their natural operation upon the climate and weather, nor will he undertake to predict good even to princes from any study he has made of the heavens; but he has learned from Thou's "eyes" (his external appearance), those "constant stars" (their changeless nature), enough of the art of divination to assure him that "truth and beauty" (Thou and You) shall succeed in producing a work worthy of them, if "from thyself to store thou wouldst convert" (if in his thoughts he can demonstrate Thou (Truth) in his labors correctly). If not, then he prophesies that in failing to do so, "Truth and Beauty" (Thou and You) will find their "doom" (they will not be used in the same manner by any one else, and the world will fail to derive any benefit from their conjoint presentation).

SONNET 15.

When I consider everything that grows
Holds in perfection but a little moment,
That this huge state presenteth naught but shows
Whereon the stars in secret influence comment;
When I perceive that men as plants increase,
Cheered and check'd even by the self-same sky,

Vaunt in their youthful sap, at height decrease,
And wear their brave state out of memory;
Then the conceit of this inconstant stay
Sets You most rich in youth before my sight,
Where wasteful time debateth with decay,
To change Your day of youth to sullied night;
  And all in war with Time, for love of You,
  As he takes from You, I engraft You new.

All things growing on this earth, after arriving at a state of "perfection" (maturity), by some "secret influence" (operation of nature), begin to decline. They hold that state but a little moment (brief period). Men grow and decrease, without any change in their surrounding conditions, one day full of youth and life, the next worn with disease or age. "Wasteful time debateth with decay" (time wears out everything that has life). "Your day of youth" (the beautiful thoughts of his early life) are now full of vigor, and he (the poet), anxious to prevent a fate for them like that he has depicted of other things, is "all in war with Time, for love of You" (is determined to accomplish his work, and embellish it with Beauty), and as Time "takes from You (Beauty), I engraft You new" (that is, he will follow one work with another as fast as possible). This, with little variation, is the same promise he made to Thou in the twelfth stanza, and conveys the additional meaning that Beauty will be reproduced from time to time as occasion may require.

SONNET 16.

But wherefore do not You a mightier way
Make war upon this bloody tyrant, Time?
And fortify Yourself in Your decay
With means more blessed than my barren rhyme?
Now stand You on the top of happy hours,
And many maiden gardens, yet unset,
With virtuous wish would bear Your living flowers,
Much liker than Your painted counterfeit;
So should the lines of life that life repair,
Which this Time's pencil or my pupil pen,
Neither in inward worth, nor outward fair,
Can make You live yourself in eyes of men.
To give away Yourself keeps Yourself still,
And You must live, drawn by Your own sweet skill.

Continuing this address to You (Beauty), the question put in the opening lines of this stanza implies that there is work for him of much greater import than any yet suggested,—work that will "fortify Yourself in Your decay" (empower him to resist the tendencies to destruction), by an exhibition of might much greater than "my barren rhyme" (the Sonnets) affords. He is now standing "on the top of happy hours" (when youth is to be exchanged for manhood). "And many maiden gardens, yet unset" (many beautiful subjects that have never been delineated), "with virtuous wish would bear Your living flowers" (if studied with truthful purpose, would unfold themselves into beautiful thoughts). Their life and bloom would exceed "your painted counterfeit" (all that has been promised for him by others). "So should the lines of life that life repair" (his future life should justify these promises). But neither (they), "this Time's pencil," nor "my pupil pen" (these rhymes of his youth), "can make You live Yourself in eyes of men" (can give him personal celebrity). "To give away Yourself keeps Yourself still" (he must adorn truth with his beauty in order that he may live). "And you must live drawn by your own sweet skill" (renown and immortality will depend upon the products of his own powers of fancy and embellishment).

Sonnet 17.

Who will believe my verse in time to come,
If it were fill'd with Your most high deserts?
Though yet, Heaven knows, it is but as a tomb
Which hides Your life, and shows not half Your parts.
If I could write the beauty of Your eyes,
And in fresh numbers number all Your graces,
The age to come would say, "This poet lies,
Such heavenly touches ne'er touch'd earthly faces,"
So should my papers, yellow'd with their age,
Be scorn'd, like old men of less truth than tongue;
And Your true rights be term'd a poet's rage,
And stretched metre of an antique song;
But were some child of yours alive that time,
You should live twice, — in it and in my rhyme.

He suggests the improbability of any future fame for Beauty, in the praise which may be bestowed upon him by "my verse" (the Sonnets); but "Heaven knows," he continues, "it is but as a tomb, which hides Your life, and shows not half Your parts." The meaning of this is very clear.

The Sonnets, by the Key used in their composition, are intended to conceal, as in "a tomb" (from the knowledge of the world), "the life" (the true origin of the dramas attributed to Shakespeare), and "show not half the parts" (show enough to excite the curiosity of the world to know their real meaning, and no more). What more probable solution than this can be given to these lines? If correct, why should Shakespeare, who appears as the author of both Sonnets and Dramas, have written them? What had he to conceal from the world that rendered the Sonnets necessary? The poet returns from this digression to further consider the argument of improbability with which he began the stanza. However laudatory might be his praises of the beauty of his "eyes" (his outward appearance), or if even in "fresh numbers" (in another poem) he should "number all his graces" (detail the powers of his genius), the future age would accuse him of lying, and say that no person was ever so richly endowed. His records would be held in the same contempt of old romancers, and denounced as the vagarics of a crazy poet. (But if some work adorned by You (Beauty), should be in existence then), "some child of yours alive that time," then the world, seeing You in that, would believe my rhyme, and You would live in both.

The symbols of marriage as the means of perpetuity, and of a child as the production of an immortal work, are dismissed from the poem in the seventeenth stanza. Inferentially, Thou (Truth), Thy (Thought), and You (Beauty) have consented to work together.

SONNET 18.

Shall I compare Thee to a summer's day?
Thou art more lovely and more temperate:
Rough winds do shake the darling buds of May,
And summer's lease hath all too short a date;
Some time too hot the eye of heaven shines,
And often is his gold complexion dimm'd;
And every fair from fair some time declines,
By chance, or nature's changing course, untrimm'd;
But Thy eternal summer shall not fade,
Nor lose possession of that fair Thou owest;
Nor shall death brag Thou wander'st in his shade,
When in eternal lines to time Thou growest:
So long as men can breathe or eyes can see,
So long lives this, and this gives life to Thee.

Thee (Thought) is compared to summer, but Thou (Truth) will be found "more lovely" (possessed of greater attractions), and "more temperate" (not changeable). Summer is subject to "rough winds," and of too brief duration. The sun is often too hot,—often overcast. Everything beautiful in nature is more or less affected by chance. Nature herself, being changeful in her course, promotes or destroys beauty, and there is no reliability to be placed upon her favors. But Thy (Thought) lives in an unfading, eternal summer, and is subject to no changes. The poet assures him that he shall not "lose possession of that fair Thou owest" (he will never separate him from Truth and Beauty in his works). They shall be immortal "when in eternal lines to time Thou growest" (when those works founded upon Truth, and decorated with Beauty, shall be produced and appreciated). They will live while men live and (have the ability) "can see" to read them, and this poem will give life sooner or later to "Thee" (Thought), their author.

SONNET 19.

Devouring Time, blunt Thou the lion's paws,
And make the earth devour her own sweet brood;
Pluck the keen teeth from the fierce tiger's jaws,
And burn the long-liv'd phœnix in her blood;
Make glad and sorry seasons as Thou fleets,
And do whate'er Thou wilt, swift-footed Time,
To the wide world, and all her fading sweets;
But I forbid Thee one most heinous crime:
O, carve not with Thy hours My Love's fair brow,
Nor draw no lines there with Thine antique pen;
Him in Thy course untainted do allow,
For Beauty's pattern to succeeding men.
Yet, do Thy worst, old Time; despite Thy wrong,
My Love shall in my verse ever live young.

The devastations wrought by Time upon animate and inanimate nature are graphically depicted in this stanza, for the purpose of showing by contrast the indestructibility of the works he has in contemplation. While Time brings an end to the fiercest and strongest animals, and "devours" the earth's "sweet brood" (human beings), it spares the records of genius,—and as they are spared, so will "My Love's fair brow" (these works of his) be spared to be "Beauty's pattern to succeeding men" (to be admired and imitated throughout all ages). Let Time "do its worst" (let them be overlooked or neglected). "Despite Thy wrong" nothing can deprive "My Love" (his dramas) of immortal youth and life.

Sonnet 20.

A woman's face, with Nature's own hand painted,
Hast Thou, the master-mistress of my passion;
A woman's gentle heart, but not acquainted
With shifting change, as is false women's fashion;
An eye more bright than theirs, less false in rolling,
Gilding the object whereupon it gazeth;
A man in hue, all hues in his controlling,
Which steals men's eyes, and women's souls amazeth.
And for a woman wert Thou first created;
Till Nature, as she wrought Thee, fell a-doting,
And by addition me of Thee defeated,
By adding one thing to my purpose nothing.
  But since she prick'd Thee out for women's pleasure,
  Mine be Thy love, and Thy love's use their treasure.

This stanza describes Thou (Truth). "A woman's face" (the attractiveness of Truth has all the charm and sweetness that is depicted in the female countenance), "by Nature's own hand painted" (undisguised by art and external ornament), "hast Thou, the master-mistress of my passion" (Truth, partaking of all the good qualities of both man and woman, forms the great subject he intends to delineate in his works). "A woman's gentle heart" (Truth, like a lovely woman, reflects nothing that is wrong or wicked, but unlike a woman, never changes). Its "eye more bright than theirs, less false in rolling" (is observant of all things, and never deceived or deceiving). "Gilding the object whereupon it gazeth" (enriching every subject it investigates). "A man in hue, all hues in his controlling" (resembling man in influence and achievements). "Which steals men's eyes, and women's souls amazeth" (commanding the observations of men and the wonder of women). "And for a woman wert Thou first created" (the eyes of the woman, after partaking of the forbidden fruit, were first opened to a knowledge of good and evil, and Truth, as the creation of that moment, was first beheld by her), but "Nature as she wrought Thee fell a-doting, and by addition me of Thee defeated" (man was added to woman in the same crime, and thus lost his truth at the moment he discovered it). "But since she prick'd Thee out for women's pleasure" (the pleasure of eating the fruit by the woman gave Truth its development), "Mine be Thy love, and Thy love's use their treasure" (his thoughts will be true, and that Truth shall give them immortality).

SONNET 21.

So is it not with me as with that Muse,
Stirr'd by a painted beauty to his verse,
Who heaven itself for ornament doth use,
And every fair with his fair doth rehearse;

Making a couplement of proud compare,
With sun and moon, with earth and sea's rich gems,
With April's first-born flowers, and all things rare
That heaven's air in this huge rondure hems.
O, let me, true in love, but truly write,
And then believe me, My Love is as fair
As any mother's child, though not so bright
As those gold candles fix'd in heaven's air:
  Let them say more that like of hearsay well;
  I will not praise, that purpose not to sell.

The poet in this stanza declares that his purpose is to write the truth. He will not imitate a contemporary pen, who is "stirr'd by a painted beauty to his verse" (chosen some subject that is out of the range of nature), and who uses all things in heaven and earth for his ornaments, showing by comparison how much the sun, moon, sea, and first flowers of spring are excelled by this subject of his verse. If the poet succeeds in drawing his characters true to life, then "My Love is as fair as any mother's child" (his dramas will be as attractive and beautiful as the symbolic child, their prototype in the first seventeen stanzas). The motive which governs him in writing is to benefit his age by delineating truth, and not to manufacture some ephemeral effusions to please the taste of the time. It is impossible at this distance of time to designate with certainty any single writer of Elizabeth's time, as the one alluded to by the poet. Many of the characters in the "Fairie Queen" would seem to indicate it might have been Spenser. His Red Cross Knight personated

Holiness; his Sir Guyon, Temperance; his Britomartis, Chastity;—while of his earthly characters "Gloriana and Belphœbe were both symbolical of Queen Elizabeth," and the character of "Envy is intended to glance at the unfortunate Mary Queen of Scots." Chambers says:—

"His inexhaustible powers of circumstantial description betrayed him into a tedious minuteness, which sometimes in the delineation of his personified passion becomes repulsive, and in the painting of natural objects led him to group together trees and plants, and assemble sounds and instruments which were never seen or heard in unison outside of fairy land. . . . . We surrender ourselves up for a time to the power of the enchanter, and witness with wonder and delight his marvellous achievements, but we wish to return again to the world, and to mingle with our fellow-mortals in its busy and passionate pursuits. It is here that Shakespeare eclipses Spenser; here that he builds upon his beautiful groundwork of fancy,—the high and durable structure of conscious dramatic truth and living reality."

Sonnet 22.

My glass shall not persuade me I am old,
So long as youth and Thou are of one date;
But when in Thee time's furrows I behold,
Then look I death my days should expiate.
For all that beauty that doth cover Thee
Is but the seemly raiment of my heart,
Which in Thy breast doth live, as Thine in me:
How can I, then, be elder than Thou art?

O, therefore, love, be of Thyself so wary,
As I, not for Myself, but for Thee will;
Bearing Thy heart, which I will keep so chary
As tender nurse her babe from faring ill.
Presume not on Thy heart when Mine is slain;
Thou gav'st Me Thine, not to give back again.

In this stanza the poet claims a conscious equality with Truth, in those powers needful for his delineation. "My glass shall not persuade me I am old, so long as youth and Thou are of one date" (nothing in his life as it passes shall discourage him in his thoughts, while they reflect truth with vigor). "But when in Thee time's furrows I behold, then look I death my days should expiate" (when they fail of faithful representation, he will abandon work). He is conscious of power to represent Truth in beautiful colors. It pervades and animates his entire being; and he cannot "be elder than Thou art" (cannot fail through any want of ability). But he must protect his thoughts from exposure for the sake of Truth. If the queen, his uncle, Lord Burleigh, or his enemy and rival, Sir Edward Coke, or any of the noblemen composing the court of Elizabeth, should ascertain that he was writing plays, he would be forced to cease. It would require such care as a "tender nurse" bestows upon a babe, to escape their observant eyes. If his heart "is slain" (if his dramatic writings are discovered), his thoughts will be lost to the world, and the grand work he has undertaken will come to an end.

SONNET 23.

As an unperfect actor on the stage,
Who with his fear is put besides his part,
Or some fierce thing replete with too much rage,
Whose strength's abundance weakens his own heart;
So I, for fear of trust, forget to say
The perfect ceremony of love's rite.
And in Mine own love's strength seem to decay,
O'ercharg'd with burden of Mine own love's might.
O, let my books be, then, the eloquence
And dumb presagers of My speaking breast;
Who plead for love and look for recompense,
More than that tongue that more hath more express'd
O, learn to read what silent love hath writ;
To hear with eyes belongs to love's fine wit.

He explains the diffidence with which he enters upon the work of composition. It is like the fear that disturbs an actor who attempts the performance of a part not perfectly committed, like something which seemingly exceeds his powers of delineation. He hesitates to write what his feelings dictate, and then in his own view "seems to decay" (to come short of his purpose), because of the magnitude which the subject assumes as it progresses. "O'ercharg'd with burden of Mine own love's might" (in this exigency his works must declare his success or failure). They are "the dumb presagers of his speaking breast" (they tell in words what he has conceived in silence). They "plead for love and look for recompense" (they will recommend themselves, and be appreciated for what they contain). "More than that tongue that more hath more express'd."

This line, in the words "that more hath more express'd," probably refers to some of the philosophical works of Bacon, in which he had *more* fully set forth the benefits of Truth. The reference is distinct enough to justify such a conclusion. The last couplet conveys the idea that his readers must be satisfied with his works, without knowing by whom they were written, as it will require "love's fine wit" to find him out by observation. Two of his plays (the Contention of York and Lancaster, and the True Tragedy of the Duke of York, afterwards changed to the second and third parts of Henry VI.) appeared without the name of Shakespeare or any other name as author, and but eleven of them were published with Shakespeare's name during his life. All the others attributed to him first appeared as of his authorship in the folio of 1623, some seven years after his death.

SONNET 24.

Mine eye hath play'd the painter, and hath stell'd
Thy beauty's form in table of My heart;
My body is the frame wherein 't is held,
And perspective it is best painter's art.
For through the painter must You see his skill,
To find where Your true image pictur'd lies;
Which in My bosom's shop is hanging still,
That hath his windows glazed with Thine eyes.
Now see what good turns eyes for eyes have done:
Mine eyes have drawn Thy shape, and Thine for me
Are windows to My breast, where-through the sun
Delights to peep, to gaze therein on Thee;
Yet eyes this cunning want to grace their art, —
They draw but what they see, know not the heart.

The first step in the preparation of a drama is outlined in this stanza: "Mine eye hath play'd the painter, and hath stell'd thy beauty's form in table of my heart" (he has thought his subject into form, and graven it upon his memory). "My body is the frame wherein 't is held" (it has not been written, but he is inspired with it). He sees it in perspective as a work of which this first conception is the most difficult part, for through the conception he can learn where it should be adorned in the composition. The picture (in his fancy), "bosom's shop," is to be illuminated by Truth; thus having furnished the creation, he subjects it to a philosophical, truthful consideration, or, in the language of the stanza, "Mine eyes have drawn Thy shape, and Thine (Truth) for me are windows to My breast, where-through the sun delights to peep, to gaze therein on Thee" (on his thoughts). But this is only a commencement. This consideration in itself is superficial. It must be followed by another that will reveal "the heart" (the inner nature).

Sonnet 25.

Let those who are in favour with their stars,
Of public honour and proud titles boast,
Whilst I, whom fortune of such triumph bars,
Unlook'd for joy in that I honour most.
Great princes' favourites their fair leaves spread
But as the marigold at the sun's eye,
And in themselves their pride lies buried,
For at a frown they in their glory die.

The painful warrior famoused for fight,
After a thousand victories once foil'd,
Is from the book of honour razed quite,
And all the rest forgot for which he toil'd:
Then happy I, that love and am belov'd,
Where I may not remove, nor be remov'd.

In this stanza he contrasts the delight which he derives from the delineation of Truth in dramatic composition, with that enjoyed by those who are honored with titles and favored by their sovereign. While they enjoy these princely favors, the fruit of much toil, and personal consideration, he enjoys a pursuit that has come to him unsought. They, like the marigold which wilts in the excessive heat of the sun, die in the height of their renown, at a frown from their sovereign. The gallant soldier, who has been successful on a thousand battle-fields, is shorn of his glory in a moment, and his great achievements, as well as he himself, forgotten. How much happier is he in an occupation suited to his taste, and subject to none of these terrible reverses!

Sonnet 26.

Lord of My Love, to whom in vassalage
Thy merit hath my duty strongly knit,
To Thee I send this written embassage,
To witness duty, not to show My wit:
Duty so great, which wit so poor as Mine
May make seem bare, in wanting words to show it,
But that I hope some good conceit of Thine
In Thy soul's thought, all naked, will bestow it;

Till whatsoever star that guides My moving
Points on me graciously with fair aspect,
And puts apparel on My tatter'd loving,
To show me worthy of Thy sweet respect:
  Then may I dare to boast how I do love Thee;
  Till then, not show My head where Thou mayst prove me.

The second step in the process of composing a drama is described in this stanza. "Lord of my love." Thou (Truth) is the impersonation, or more properly the attribute, of his own nature, that he addresses. He is the lord of "my love," and "my love" is his dramas, the product of his labors. As fast as a new drama is completed, it is added to the impersonation which he calls "my love." Thou is his "vassal" (servant), and being Truth, he is from dutiful consideration conjoined to him. In pursuance of that duty, he submits to him "this written embassage" (the truths which he intends to illustrate in his dramas). They are evidently bare, disconnected, separate, and "wanting words" (void of individuality to show their meaning). But Thou will conceive a plan "in Thy soul's thought" (in his thoughts), and "all naked will bestow it" (and not impair its purity). Then the "star that guides My moving" (his powers of expression) will "put apparel on My tatter'd loving" (will dress it in words and figures), which will be approved by Thy (Thought). Then he will be willing that the world should see it, but "till then not show My head where Thou (Truth) mayst prove me." (Until the composition is completed, he will keep it concealed, lest in these "tatters," gathered from the writers of past ages, he (the writer) will be exposed as a plagiarist and thief, and thereby deprive the dramas of the influence and effect intended for them in their creation.)

Archbishop Tenison, who was really the literary executor of Bacon, found among his papers one bearing the title of "Ornamenta Rationalia, a collection of certain weighty and elegant sentences." The collection of sentences, which had evidently been at some former time enclosed in this paper, were never found. It is fair to presume, from the title given them (Ornaments of Truth), that they had served the purpose designed for them, and been destroyed. This collection and the Promus probably constituted that "tatter'd loving" referred to in the stanza.

SONNET 27.

Weary with toil I haste Me to My bed,
The dear repose for limbs with travel tir'd,
But then begins a journey in My head,
To work My mind, when body's work 's expir'd;
For then My thoughts, from far where I abide,
Intend a zealous pilgrimage to Thee,
And keep My drooping eyelids open wide,
Looking on darkness, which the blind do see:
Save that My soul's imaginary sight
Presents Thy shadow to My sightless view,
Which, like a jewel hung in ghastly night,
Makes black night beauteous, and her old face new.
Lo, thus, by day My limbs, by night My mind,
For Thee and for Myself no quiet find.

The work of composition is still progressing. Bacon, at the period of his life which this stanza prefigures, was a young man, pursuing his legal studies at Gray's Inn. He was very studious, and "encountered and subdued the difficulties and obscurities of the science in which he was doomed to labor." It was after the daily "toil" which this course of life imposed, and he had retired to his "bed," that there would begin "a journey in My head to work My mind" (he would contemplate, arrange, and fill up the parts of his drama). His thoughts would lead him "from far where I abide" (to the countries and cities where his scenes were located) on a "zealous pilgrimage to Thee" (with Thought alone for his guide). Despite the "darkness" of his chamber, he was kept awake, and his imagination presented Thought to him in such variety, that, like a diamond, it shone through the darkness, and illuminated the night with beauty, giving to all around a new appearance. The unceasing labor of body by day, and Thought by night, gave no rest to him, or to Thought.

SONNET 28.

How can I, then, return in happy plight,
That am debarr'd the benefit of rest?
When day's oppression is not eas'd by night,
But day by night, and night by day, oppress'd?
And each, though enemies to either's reign,
Do in consent shake hands to torture Me;
The one by toil, the other to complain
How far I toil, still farther off from Thee.

I tell the day, to please him Thou are bright
And dost him grace when clouds do blot the heaven:
So flatter I the swart-complexion'd night,
When sparkling stars twire not Thou glid'st the even.
  But day doth daily draw My sorrows longer,
  And night doth nightly make grief's strength seem stronger.

The care and anxiety inseparable from these labors are described in this stanza. He is so worn in both body and mind, for want of repose, that he cannot preserve his customary deportment or amiability. The toil of the day is unrelieved by sleep, and the thoughts which usurp his slumbers render the day burdensome. Day and night are equally heavy,—one by the labor it brings, the other by the perplexities which fill his thoughts. All efforts of his to reconcile these afflictions are thwarted by the consciousness that the day's work is unsuited to his nature, and hateful in his eyes; while the work at night is constantly presenting new difficulties,—making "grief's strength seem stronger."

Sonnet 29.

When, in disgrace with fortune and men's eyes,
I all alone beweep My outcast state,
And trouble deaf heaven with My bootless cries,
And look upon Myself and curse My fate,
Wishing Me like to one more rich in hope,
Featur'd like him, like him with friends possess'd,
Desiring this man's art and that man's scope,
With what I most enjoy contented least;
Yet in these thoughts Myself almost despising,
Haply I think on Thee, and then My state

(Like to the lark at break of day arising)
From sullen earth sings hymns at heaven's gate:
For Thy sweet love remember'd such wealth brings,
That then I scorn to change My state with kings.

The poignancy of grief expressed in this stanza singularly illustrates what we may conceive to have been the condition of so sensitive a person as Lord Bacon, when by the death of his father he was recalled from France, and forced to make choice of a pursuit (the law) repugnant to him as the only means of obtaining a livelihood. He was "in disgrace with fortune" (without means) "and men's eyes (unappreciated)." His state, from being that of a child petted by the queen and nobility on account of his high birth, was changed to that of a young man whose only prospect for success in life depended upon the kindness of relatives and friends in official position at the court of Elizabeth. His tastes and studies were philosophical, and until this misfortune came, he expected to devote his life to sedentary pursuits and the study of nature. Nothing now was left him but a choice between the law, which he hated, and a position as an officer of the realm. With the hope of obtaining the one, he gave faithful but unwilling service to the other. His life at Gray's Inn was reclusive, and his relatives were cold and unapproachable. That he should feel himself to be an "outcast" was not surprising, and that all the experience described in the stanza should have been his was but a natural result of the great disappointment which had made such changes in his plans and hopes. His ardent prayers were to a "deaf heaven" (not answered). No regrets could change his lot. He saw his cousin, Robert Cecil, son of Lord Burleigh, favored by gifts and laden with honors by the queen, as he would have been had his father lived. Though he might wish for the same privileges, for the same resources, for the same friends, and desire their aid, their facilities, their powers, they would not come at his bidding. (He was discontented with the pursuit he had been forced to adopt), "with what I most enjoy contented least." In this state, he undoubtedly felt "myself almost despising (that his life was of little use to himself)." With no recreation to break the gloom of these and like reflections, he was led to consider the variety, scope, and beauty of his own thoughts, and they had enkindled in him the idea of presenting Truth in character, in dramatic composition. That resource was an abundant antidote. While engaged in that he was happy. Like the lark in his morning song, he could sing a heavenly song, and he would not exchange the pleasure it afforded him for all the splendor of the court.

A thoughtful consideration of this and several of the succeeding stanzas of this poem, especially of the closing couplet,—

> "For Thy sweet love remember'd such wealth brings,
> That then I scorn to change My state with kings,"

has led me to believe that they are intended to convey a double meaning. Most of the time while at Gray's Inn, Bacon was in straitened circumstances, owing to his extravagant habits. His life, as gathered from the letters which passed between himself and his mother, published in Mr. Dixon's book, shows that she was at times put to great straits to raise money to relieve him and his brother Anthony from foolish debts. She is constantly warning him against contracting them. He was also at this time fond of the theatre, and took part as an amateur in one or more masks and plays which he had aided in composing for special occasions. This poem in its further developments will show that very soon after he began to compose his dramas he conveyed them, authorship and all, to Shakespeare. This must have been in pursuance of some previous understanding of longer or shorter date; and in view thereof, it is not improbable that at this very time he was sharing with Shakespeare in his receipts from Blackfriars Theatre.

In the twenty-first stanza, after speaking of other poets, he says:—

> "Let them say more that like of hearsay well;
> I will not praise that purpose not to sell."

He must have seen then as well as afterwards that he could not figure in the court of Elizabeth as a playwright, lawyer, and statesman. Yet "he purposed not to sell," but he had previously, in all probability, purposed to make his writings a source of revenue, which was accomplished by a different arrangement. This subject will be considered at greater length in the light of stronger facts hereafter disclosed.

SONNET 30.

When to the sessions of sweet silent thought
I summon up remembrance of things past,
I sigh the lack of many a thing I sought,
And with old woes new wail my dear time's waste:
Then can I drown an eye (unus'd to flow),
For precious friends hid in death's dateless night,
And weep afresh love's long since cancell'd woe,
And moan the expense of many a vanish'd sight;
Then can I grieve at grievances foregone,
And heavily from woe to woe tell o'er
The sad account of fore-bemoaned moan,
Which I new pay as if not paid before.
But if the while I think on Thee (dear friend)
All losses are restor'd and sorrows end.

The retrospect of his life in this stanza but sharpens his sorrows. The life he had prefigured for himself, in earlier and more fortunate days, had not been realized. Many privileges and enjoyments which he had then anticipated never came to him. One grief had followed another all the way: first he mourned the loss of "precious friends" (his father and others who would have assisted him), then "love's long since cancell'd woe" (probably a sweetheart who had died, or mayhap jilted him), then "many a vanished sight" (his early home and its associations, the kindness of the queen and nobility). These had given place to an obscure life of study and monotony at Gray's Inn. These early trials and disappointments increased his despondency and saddened his life. He sought and found ample relief from these troubles in the world of his own creation,—the truth, beauty, and character he was delineating in his dramas.

Another interpretation of this stanza would seem to point to his wants as a student. He "sighs the lack of many things he sought" (he is in want of books, furniture, clothing, means of enjoyment). Much of his time, which would be given to study were he thus supplied, is lost, to his great regret. Those old "friends" (his books) have been gone for years, and the privileges he once enjoyed have vanished. He has been compelled to contract debts, the "sad account" of which has greatly distressed him. But his "dear friend" (Shakespeare) having come to his relief, he is enabled to purchase such things as are needed, and all "sorrows end."

SONNET 31.

Thy bosom is endeared with all hearts,
Which I by lacking have supposed dead,
And there reigns love, and all love's loving parts,
And all those friends which I thought buried.
How many a holy and obsequious tear
Hath dear religious love stolen from Mine eye
As interest of the dead, which now appear
But things remov'd that hidden in Thee lie!

Thou art the grave where buried love doth live,
Hung with the trophies of My lovers gone,
Who all their parts of me to Thee did give;
That due of many now is Thine alone:
  Their images I lov'd I view in Thee,
  And Thou (all they) hast all the all of Me.

Thy (Thought), in this stanza, is represented as directing his attention to the stories and tales he had read in his youth. They were the "hearts which I by lacking have supposed dead" (he had dismissed them from his thoughts as one who, after reading, dismisses a novel). The search for a subject to dramatize had revived the memory of them. They furnished the framework of his great creations in illustrating Truth, and thus became to him "love and all love's loving parts." He remembered how they affected him when he first read them, but now that he could make a better use of them, they seemed to him as "things removed that hidden in Thee lie" (as things which had remained unnoticed in his memory, until, while seeking for parts to illustrate the truth he had in view, like hidden things they came to light). When examined he found that by dressing them in his own thoughts and fancy, they were the materials he most needed; they furnished truth, beauty, and parts. The "images" he saw in them in youth came back to his thoughts now, and he adopted them as the subjects of his dramas. We need look no further for the motives which led him to adapt his plays from the stories of former ages.

SONNET 32.

If Thou survive My well-contented day,
When that churl Death My bones with dust shall cover,
And shalt by fortune once more re-survey
These poor rude lines of Thy deceased lover,
Compare them with the bettering of the time,
And though they be outstripp'd by every pen,
Reserve them for My Love, not for their rhyme,
Exceeded by the height of happier men.
O, then vouchsafe me but this loving thought:
"Had My friend's Muse grown with his growing age,
A dearer birth than this his love had brought,
To march in ranks of better equipage;
But since he died, and poets better prove,
Theirs for their style I 'll read, His for His Love."

The object of this stanza is to direct those who, in after generations, should seek for the meaning of this poem, to study it, not for any beauty in its composition, but solely to discover who was its author. There is very little to admire in its style, as compared with the works of the poets of succeeding ages, therefore "reserve them for My Love, not for their rhyme" (My Love personated his dramas). Study them to ascertain who Shakespeare was, and who I am. Think, if you please, that if I had lived and cultivated my powers I would have written better, but as I did not, and your poets excel me, give no heed to my style, but read my poem to ascertain the meaning of the history it contains. One readily infers from this that Bacon appreciated his dramatic writings at their full worth, and derived great delight from the thought that future ages would discover that he was their author, and do justice to his memory.

SONNET 33.

Full many a glorious morning have I seen
Flatter the mountain-tops with sovereign eye,
Kissing with golden face the meadows green,
Gilding pale streams with heavenly alchemy;
Anon permit the basest clouds to ride
With ugly rack on his celestial face,
And from the forlorn world his visage hide,
Stealing unseen to west with this disgrace:
Even so My sun one early morn did shine,
With all-triumphant splendour on My brow;
But out, alack! he was but one hour Mine,
The region cloud hath mask'd him from Me now.
  Yet him for this My Love no whit disdaineth;
  Suns of the world may stain, when heaven's sun staineth.

This majestic verse fittingly describes his brief hour of enjoyment when his first drama ("My sun") was completed. It is very beautiful. As the sun which renders the morning glorious by flattering the mountain-tops, kissing the green meadows, and gilding the pale streams with its rays, is suddenly obscured by dark clouds, until its setting, so his sun one "early morn did shine with all-triumphant splendour on my brow" (he had triumphed over all difficulties in the composition of his work, and brought it to completion). It was like the glory of morning sunlight to him. Alas! "he was but one hour Mine" (he was obliged by his position in life to give it, with all its beauty, to another). "The region cloud hath mask'd him from me now" (his right to it was like that of one who concealed his person and features with a mask to escape recognition). Shakespeare, "the region cloud," stood between him and that sun at that moment, and has masked him from the world ever since. Yet "My Love" (his drama) was no more affected by this change over the earthly sun than the earth by the clouds that hid the heavenly sun. The darkness was all to him alone.

SONNET 34.

Why didst Thou promise such a beauteous day,
And make me travel forth without My cloak,
To let base clouds o'ertake Me in My way,
Hiding Thy bravery in their rotten smoke?
'T is not enough that through the cloud Thou break,
To dry the rain on My storm-beaten face,
For no man well of such a salve can speak
That heals the wound and cures not the disgrace:
Nor can Thy shame give physic to My grief;
Though Thou repent, yet I have still the loss:
The offender's sorrow lends but weak relief
To him that bears the strong offence's cross.
  Ah! but those tears are pearl which Thy love sheds,
  And they are rich and ransom all ill deeds.

He tells in this stanza how he became dispossessed of his dramas. As if angry with Thou (Truth), he asks why the promise was made of so much fame in his work, as he was to lose it all so soon. He was in distress for means to live, "without my cloak," and possibly threatened with arrest, "base clouds" overtook him on his way. In this extremity it occurred to him that he might dispose of his play to some theatrical manager. Shakespeare, a young fellow in pursuit of fortune, was at the time a shareholder in Blackfriars Theatre. Thou's (Truth's) "bravery" (Truth's incorruptibility) was hid "in the rotten smoke" of the clouds (in the unpleasant embarrassments that were threatening the author). Bacon found Shakespeare, and arranged with him to assume authorship of the drama. The sacrifice was made with less reluctance, because he could not, without destroying all his future prospects, be known as the writer of plays for the theatre. The play thus disposed of was probably "The History of the Contention between the Houses of Lancaster and York," his first effort. It was afterwards incorporated in the play of Henry VI. We learn from the history of the dramas that this play and the "True Tragedy of the Duke of York" were performed before the poems of "Venus and Adonis" and "Lucrece" were published, of both of which Shakespeare appeared as author. This play was first published without the name of an author, but Green, who by many critics is supposed to have aided in its composition, alludes unmistakably to Shakespeare as connected with it, in his "Groatesworth of Wit." This arrangement probably marks the period, not later than 1592, when the friendship commenced between Bacon and Shakespeare.

It appears from this stanza that the arrangement was of Bacon's own seeking. Allegorically he charges the offence to that attribute of himself, Thou (Truth), because it was untruthful to permit the play to appear as Shakespeare's. During the transaction Thou is represented as breaking through the clouds with a smile of encouragement, which, while it "heals the wound" (sanctions the act), "cures not the disgrace" (does not relieve him of the shame). Then the address changes to "Thy's shame," or the wrong done to his own thoughts, which he sees in Shakespeare. "Nor can Thy shame give physic to My grief" (Shakespeare's part in the purchase did not remove any of the offensive features of the act). Any delicacy he might feel in assuming the authorship did not restore the play to the true writer of it. It was gone from him forever. There was this consolation: "Those tears are pearl which Thy love sheds" (he has received substantial pay for the play). "And they are rich and ransom all ill deeds" (and that compensates for all that is wrong in the transaction between them).

SONNET 35.

No more be griev'd at that which Thou hast done:
Roses have thorns, and silver fountains mud;
Clouds and eclipses stain both moon and sun,
And loathsome canker lives in sweetest bud.
All men make faults, and even I in this,
Authorizing Thy trespass with compare,

Myself corrupting, salving Thy amiss,
Excusing Thy sins more than Thy sins are;
For to Thy sensual fault I bring in sense, —
Thy adverse party is Thy advocate, —
And 'gainst Myself a lawful plea commence.
Such civil war is in My love and hate
That I an accessary needs must be
To that sweet thief which sourly robs from Me.

In this stanza he clears up any possible doubt of the meaning of the previous stanza, and virtually acknowledges the arrangement to have been of his own seeking. Thou (Truth) is told not to grieve, as his offence is a very natural one. It is no worse than a thorn to a rose, mud to a silver fountain, or canker to a bud. So also of the shame of Shakespeare. Your fault is no worse than the faults which all men make. By authorizing it, he (Bacon) has corrupted himself, and is more to be despised than Shakespeare, whose fault appears greater than it really is. The sensual or shameful part of it he alone is responsible for, as the conflict in his feelings has necessarily made him the "accessary" of Thou, "that sweet thief," in the arrangement. In plainer phrase, he is the only person blamable in the affair.

SONNET 36.

Let Me confess that we two must be twain,
Although our undivided loves are one;
So shall those blots that do with Me remain,
Without Thy help, by Me be borne alone.

In our two loves there is but one respect,
Though in our lives a separable spite,
Which though it alter not love's sole effect,
Yet doth it steal sweet hours from love's delight.
I may not evermore acknowledge Thee,
Lest My bewailed guilt should do Thee shame;
Nor Thou with public kindness honour Me,
Unless Thou take that honour from Thy name;
  But do not so; I love Thee in such sort
  As, Thou being Mine, Mine is Thy good report.

In this and the three following stanzas, addressed to Thy (Thought), he tells him what his plan is for concealing from the public the part he is to play in the composition of the dramas. He and Shakespeare must live divided ("be twain"), in other words, they must live as if strangers to each other. Their objects ("loves") are of course undivided. But by this arrangement, none of the stains which affect him now, or none that he may hereafter incur, will ever reach Shakespeare or the dramas. Their object in common is to compose and present the plays. It is a business,—a partnership, nothing more. In their lives there is a "separable spite" (Bacon is a lawyer of noble family, soon to become a courtier, politician, statesman, and public officer, liable at any time to occupy high position, and to be ennobled by Elizabeth; Shakespeare is a young actor at Blackfriars, and his habits and occupation will forbid his access to the society of which Bacon is an ornament). This great difference in their lives and pursuits will "alter not love's sole effect" (not disturb the great object of making money in their business), whatever its influence over their social relations. A time may come when Bacon will find it necessary to ignore Shakespeare, to save him from the mishaps of his own life. He may be obliged to cease writing, and then Thou (Truth) will no longer honor him in theatrical representation, unless Thou should take the honor from Shakespeare's own labors. He advises Shakespeare against engaging in any such labors, because Thou (Truth) is his own henchman, and the plays he has written "Thy good report" (are the product of his own thoughts).

SONNET 37.

As a decrepit father takes delight
To see his active child do deeds of youth,
So I, made lame by fortune's dearest spite,
Take all My comfort of Thy worth and truth;
For whether beauty, birth, or wealth, or wit,
Or any of these all, or all, or more,
Entitled in Thy parts do crowned sit,
I make My love engrafted to this store.
So then I am not lame, poor, nor despis'd,
Whilst that this shadow doth such substance give,
That I in Thy abundance am suffic'd,
And by a part of all Thy glory live.
Look, what is best, that best I wish in Thee:
This wish I have; then ten times happy Me!

Continuing the address to Thy, he prefigures in this stanza the relationship which he wishes to fill towards Shakespeare. As a father, deprived by his infirmities from mingling in the affairs of society, takes great pleasure in the enterprise and business habits of his son, so he, "made lame by fortune's dearest spite" (cut off by the death of his father from the privileges, enjoyments, and titles which he was encouraged to anticipate in his youth), will supply their place by watchful and gratifying interest in Shakespeare's "worth and truth" (in the public appreciation of his dramas, as they appear in Shakespeare's name). By adding to their "beauty, birth, or wealth, or wit," or to any other qualities which their "parts" require, he will overcome and forget his misfortunes and deprivations. They will be a source of great delight to him as long as they afford him ample revenue. "That I in Thy abundance am suffic'd" (and his part of the proceeds affords him a livelihood), "and by a part of all Thy glory live" (as he is convinced that Shakespeare means well, is honest and true, he is more than satisfied with the arrangement they have entered into).

SONNET 38.

How can My Muse want subject to invent,
While Thou dost breathe, that pour'st into My verse
Thine own sweet argument, too excellent
For every vulgar paper to rehearse?
O, give Thyself the thanks, if aught in Me
Worthy perusal stand against Thy sight;
For who 's so dumb that cannot write to Thee,
When Thou Thyself dost give invention light?
Be Thou the tenth Muse, ten times more in worth
Than those old nine which rhymers invocate;

And he that calls on Thee, let him bring forth
Eternal numbers to outlive long date.
If My slight Muse do please these curious days,
The pain be Mine, but Thine shall be the praise.

In this stanza he tells how greatly he has been relieved in his circumstances by this partnership with Shakespeare. He can write now, and Thou (Truth), being ever ready to assist him and pour his "own sweet argument into his verse" (the history of his dramatic works into this poem), which of itself excels that of other writers, he will not want for subjects to write about, or invention. But Shakespeare may thank himself for it if the plays are a success. It is the money, and the ease and freedom from care which that brings, that empowers him to write; but it is Thou (Truth), as well as Thyself (Thought delineated), which gives "invention light" (enables him to present his dramas to the world). Thou (Truth) is the "tenth Muse"; he will "bring forth eternal numbers" (produce immortal lines). If this poem arouses any curiosity in the public, let all the sorrow it contains be his, and all the "praise" Shakespeare's.

SONNET 39.

O, how Thy worth with manners may I sing,
When Thou art all the better part of Me?
What can Mine own praise to Mine own self bring?
And what is 't but Mine own, when I praise Thee?
Even for this let us divided live,
And our dear love lose name of single one,

That by this separation I may give
That due to Thee, which Thou deserv'st alone.
O absence, what a torment wouldst Thou prove,
Were it not Thy sour leisure gave sweet leave
To entertain the time with thoughts of love,
Which time and thoughts so sweetly doth deceive,
And that Thou teachest how to make one twain,
By praising him here who doth hence remain!

Some idea of the personality of Shakespeare, and of Bacon's appreciation of him, is given in this stanza, addressed to Thy (Thought):—

"O, how thy worth with manners may I sing,
When Thou art all the better part of me?"—

is as if he had said, How can I praise his manners and speak the truth (Thou) which is uppermost in my nature? Shakespeare may have been a boor. If he praises himself, what does it amount to, now that he has virtually disclaimed the dramas, and no one can echo that praise? If he praises Shakespeare, that is simply to praise himself. For these reasons it is better they should live apart, and Bacon's name be unknown. He can then give to Shakespeare alone all the praise he deserves. Probably when writing this Bacon smiled ironically, for what praise did he deserve? This stanza was conceived in a humorous vein all the way through. After jeering at Shakespeare's manners, exposing the futility of attempting to praise himself, and the effect, as he realized it, of praising Shakespeare, and recommending their separate life that he may praise him singly as he deserves, he then says that he has during an hour of absence from work improved the "sour leisure" (the time so grudgingly taken), to fill it with "thoughts of love." The seeming meaning he has given to the thoughts has deceived or belied their real meaning,—which was simply to ridicule the arrangement between himself and Shakespeare, "praising him here who doth hence remain."

SONNET 40.

Take all My Loves, My Love, yea, take them all:
What hast Thou then more than Thou hadst before?
No love, My Love, that Thou mayst *true* love call;
All mine was Thine before Thou hadst this more.
Then if for *My Love* thou My Love receivest,
I cannot blame Thee, for *My Love* Thou usest;
But yet be blam'd, if Thou Thyself deceivest
By wilful taste of what this self refusest.
I do forgive Thy robbery, gentle thief,
Although Thou steal Thee *all my poverty;*
And yet, love knows, it is a greater grief
To bear love's wrong than hate's known injury.
  Lascivious grace, in whom all ill well shows,
  Kill me with spites; yet we must not be foes.

In this stanza Shakespeare is put in possession of his plays, and becomes virtually the author of them. "Take all My Loves, My Love" (Shakespeare now being adopted as one of his loves, he mentally as my love unites him to the plays, which he calls "My Love," and addresses him also by that endearing name, and under it invests him with the plays). In the next two lines he declares that

Thou (Truth) has gained nothing by this transfer that he can call "true love." Shakespeare, though added to "My Love," is not to be recognized as any part of the truth in the plays designated by that title. He is simply added to it. By the next line, "All mine was Thine before Thou hadst this more" (he had devoted all his dramas to Truth before he added Shakespeare, "this more," to them). By giving to Shakespeare the credence of the plays, and thus uniting him to the volume of "My Love," which was composed of truth, Thou (Truth) had become possessed of him. If Thou (Truth) will receive him as "My Love," then he may use the plays, and it will be his own fault if he makes use of any portion of them that his judgment disapproves. He is the manager, and must adapt them for proper representation. "I do forgive Thy [Thought's] robbery, gentle thief, although Thou [Truth] steal Thee all my poverty" (his only poverty in a literary sense was Shakespeare. He (Bacon) is satisfied with the arrangement, though he (Bacon) loses all that he might gain in honor and renown, by being known as their author). The changes he will make in them will be like a "lascivious grace, in whom all ill well shows" (like a well-dressed wanton; it will not be to his taste). "Kill me with spite" (but rather than quarrel about it he will not object). "We must not be foes" (because of any improprieties in this transaction).

The eighth line reads "this self" in the quarto of 1609. This, as referring back to "this more" (Shakespeare) in the fourth line, is undoubtedly correct. All modern editions have it "Thyself."

The understanding between Bacon and Shakespeare provided for the payment to Bacon of one half of the profits accruing from the plays, as appears in the thirty-seventh stanza. White says that "play-going was the favorite amusement of all the better and brighter part of the London public, gentle and simple." The profits which made Shakespeare rich must have greatly increased the meagre exchequer of Bacon. The arrangement was to continue until brighter days came to Bacon, and he could from his profession or public office reap a revenue sufficient for his wants. If that time ever came, the entire property in the dramas, authorship and all, was to vest in Shakespeare, and the arrangement would be terminated.

Sonnet 41.

Those pretty wrongs that liberty commits,
When I am sometime absent from Thy heart,
Thy beauty and Thy years full well befits,
For still temptation follows where Thou art.
Gentle Thou art, and therefore to be won,
Beauteous Thou art, therefore to be assailed;
And when a woman woos, what woman's son
Will sourly leave her till he have prevailed?
Ah Me! but yet Thou mightst my seat forbear,
And chide Thy beauty and Thy straying youth,

> Who lead Thee in their riot even there
> Where Thou art forc'd to break a twofold truth,—
> Hers, by Thy beauty tempting her to Thee,
> Thine, by Thy beauty being false to Me.

Full authority is given to Shakespeare in this stanza to make such minor changes in the thought and expression of the dramas as may be deemed necessary. "Those pretty wrongs that liberty commits" (the little alterations you find it necessary to make for the purpose of adapting them to the stage,—your own sense of propriety and grace), "Thy beauty and Thy years" (must dictate). "Temptation follows where Thou (Truth) art." Be careful not to belie the truth of the drama. Thou (Truth) can be easily "won" (preserved) or "assailed" (destroyed). "And when a woman woos" (the dramas, "My Love," are represented as a female throughout the poem, and the changes for purpose of representation, if any, are made because "My Love" (the dramas) wooed), "what woman's son will sourly leave her till he have prevailed?" (if the change is really necessary it may be made.) But as he believed he had adhered to the truth, he disliked any change, "Thou mightst my seat forbear." Your ideas of propriety and expression are crude and unpolished, and you will, he fears, mar the harmony of the play, and break a twofold truth: "Thy beauty [Thy thoughts] tempting her to Thee," and disfigure my work, "Thy beauty [My thoughts] being false to me."

SONNET 42.

That Thou hast her, it is not all My grief,
And yet it may be said I lov'd her dearly;
That she hath Thee, is of my wailing chief,
A loss in love that touches Me more nearly.
Loving offenders, thus I will excuse ye:
Thou dost love her, because Thou know'st I love her;
And for My sake even so doth she abuse Me,
Suffering My friend for My sake to approve her.
If I lose Thee, My loss is My Love's gain,
And losing her, My friend hath found that loss;
Both find each other, and I lose both twain,
And both for My sake lay on Me this cross:
  But here's the joy; My friend and I are one;
  Sweet flattery! then she loves but Me alone.

He reconciles himself to the change he has made in this stanza. He is not greatly disturbed by the part which Thou is represented to have taken, but the transfer to Shakespeare "is of his wailing chief" (is the great sacrifice). "A loss in love that touches him more nearly" (it is parting with the most cherished fruits of his own great genius, years of patient labor and study, and all the greatness, fame, and immortality they would have given to his name). He excuses Thou (Truth), because his love for the dramas (My Love) is inspired by the love he bears for them himself. "And for My sake, even so doth she abuse Me" (a similar love in "My Love," for the purpose of supplying his wants, has caused her to leave him, and "suffer My friend" (Shakespeare) for the same reason to appropriate her). He has parted with his power over the dramas to Shakespeare; "My loss," but

"My Love" (his dramas), as she is now in hands where her great lessons can receive publicity, is a gainer by it. She has left him, "losing her," (Shakespeare) "My friend," has found her, "that loss," and thus they "for his sake" (for the purpose of furnishing him with money) abandon his name. But the joy of it all is, that he (Bacon) and Shakespeare are bound to each other, and he flatters himself that "My Love" (his dramas) is as dear to him as ever.

Many, I believe most, of the writers who have reviewed these Sonnets critically, interpret the last three, 40, 41, and 42, to mean that Shakespeare's friend had robbed him of his mistress. In consideration of his youth, beauty, and susceptibility, he excused the offence, forgave him, and surrendered his mistress to his keeping. This conjecture furnishes, probably, the most natural view of the subject to one who receives Shakespeare as the true author of the poem, but it seems to me that the many transpositions and subtile changes of the thought, especially in the fortieth stanza, could never to the most acute mind have made such an interpretation satisfactory. Regarding Bacon as the author, and the story as an allegorical description of the course he pursued to conceal his authorship of the dramas, and to establish it firmly in Shakespeare, these stanzas are greatly relieved of their seeming intricacy and confusion.

SONNET 43.

When most I wink, then do Mine eyes best see,
For all the day they view things unrespected;
But when I sleep, in dreams they look on Thee,
And darkly bright are bright in dark directed.
Then Thou, whose shadow shadows doth make bright,
How would Thy shadow's form form happy show
To the clear day with Thy much clearer light,
When to unseeing eyes Thy shade shines so!
How would, I say, Mine eyes be blessed made
By looking on Thee in the living day,
When in dead night Thy fair imperfect shade
Through heavy sleep on sightless eyes doth stay!
All days are nights to see till I see Thee,
And nights bright days when dreams do show Thee me.

The partnership with Shakespeare being satisfactorily arranged, he returns to the work of composition, the process of which, though described in other words, is substantially the same as that at first adopted. (The drowsy hours of night), "when most I wink," in "sleep" and "in dreams," were the moments which gave birth to the wonderful creations of his genius,—the employments of the day were unpleasant to him. In those "darkly bright" hours, his thoughts reflected the light which directed them through all the complexities of the subjects he had chosen, and Thou (Truth) gave life to the shadows (characters), by means of which they were illustrated. In this manner, fashioned after the story chosen as a basis, his dramas were wrought into shape. Truth and Beauty were at his command, to impart to them their separate elements, and he saw them as "shadows" of the forms which in the "much clearer light" of day they would assume. The work was a passion with him, and from the moment that it entered his mind (he longed for its completion), to be "looking on Thee in the living day." The day was tedious until the night came, that he might think and work, and the nights brighter than the days, that filled his thoughts with his subject.

SONNET 44.

If the dull substance of My flesh were thought,
Injurious distance should not stop My way;
For then despite of space I would be brought,
From limits far remote, where Thou dost stay.
No matter then although My foot did stand
Upon the farthest earth remov'd from Thee,
For nimble thought can jump both sea and land
As soon as think the place where he would be.
But, ah! thought kills Me that I am not thought,
To leap large lengths of miles when Thou art gone,
But that, so much of earth and water wrought,
I must attend time's leisure with My moan,
  Receiving nought by elements so slow
  But heavy tears, badges of either's woe.

In this stanza he likens his infatuation to thought. If his body like his mind were thought, neither "space" nor "limits far remote" should separate him from his work. If he stood "upon the farthest earth remov'd from" it, he would jump the distance of "sea and land" intervening "as soon as think." But alas! his body is a solid, he cannot overcome its resistance and leap over the "earth and water" that lie between him and the subject of his passions. His days are so differently occupied, he is so far away, that he must await the leisure of evening, when other labors are over, before he can return to the recreation so full of enjoyment. It may be reasonably inferred from this allusion to "earth and water," that Bacon had some daily occupation which took him away from his lodgings at Gray's Inn. As we shall soon see, he was, if not then, at least soon after, required to be in daily attendance upon the queen. He was evidently, through some cause, unable to devote the time that he wished to the composition of his dramas.

Sonnet 45.

The other two, slight air and purging fire,
Are both with Thee, wherever I abide;
The first My thought, the other My desire,
These present-absent with swift motion slide.
For when these quicker elements are gone
In tender embassy of love to Thee,
My life, being made of four, with two alone
Sinks down to death, oppress'd with melancholy;
Until life's composition be recur'd
By those swift messengers return'd from Thee,
Who even but now come back again, assur'd
Of Thy fair health, recounting it to me.
  This told, I joy; but then no longer glad,
  I send them back again, and straight grow sad.

An advance in the composition is described in this stanza. Two other elements, air and fire, are here referred to as being always with the drama he is composing, wherever he abides. In other words, whether at Gorhambury, Twickenham, York House, or Gray's Inn, he had "slight air" (a small room for his own use), and "purging fire" (the means for warming it). His thought he likened to the one and his desire to the other. The "earth and water," as he says in the previous stanza, are the slow elements, the obstructions, but the air and fire are swift; and while they engage him in reflecting upon how best to illustrate Truth and Beauty, the other two, "My life being made of four,"— Thou (Truth), Thy (Thought), You (Beauty), and I (Bacon as an individual), he is as one dead or "oppress'd with melancholy," but when the idea is formed and the illustration seems to be perfect, and "life's composition is recur'd" by these reflections, and written in the play, he becomes elated; but immediately another process of the same kind is begun, and he is again cast down. The intention is to describe the difficulty, which not only he but every writer meets with while tasking his mind for the thoughts he wishes to use in composition.

SONNET 46.

Mine eye and heart are at a mortal war
How to divide the conquest of their sight;
Mine eye, My heart their picture's sight would bar,
My heart Mine eye the freedom of that right.
My heart doth plead that Thou in him dost lie, —
A closet never pierc'd with crystal eyes, —

But the defendant doth that plea deny,
And says in him their fair appearance lies.
To 'cide this title is impanelled
A quest of thoughts, all tenants to the heart,
And by their verdict is determined
The clear eye's moiety and the dear heart's part;
As thus: Mine eye's due is their outward part,
And My heart's right their inward love of heart.

This stanza, in the form of a lawsuit between the "eye and heart" (seeing and feeling), describes how he was affected by the first representation of his play upon the stage. "Mine eye and heart are at a mortal war how to divide the conquest of their sight" (he was unable to determine which he most admired, the scenery, acting, and mechanical effects in the representation of the play, or the philosophy, truthfulness, and sentimentality of its composition). "Mine eye, my heart their picture's sight would bar" (when seeing it acted, he gave no thought to the sentiment uttered). "My heart Mine eye the freedom of that right" (when reflecting upon it for its great power of thought and expression, he regretted its appearance in the theatre). "My heart doth plead that Thou [Truth] in him doth lie" (Truth, being the basic element of the drama, had no part in the modes of its public portrayal). "But the defendant doth that plea deny, and says in him their fair appearance lies" (the beauty of the drama, as representative of character, can only be appreciated by seeing it in theatrical display). To determine this mortal difference between seeing and feeling, a jury of thoughts is impanelled. They were "all tenants of the heart," as jurors were tenants of the vicinage or county. They were the thoughts which formed a correct judgment of the respective sensations the play as a composition and as a scenic representation was likely to excite. Their verdict was that the "eye's due is their outward part" (the exhibition on the stage), the "heart's right their inward love of heart" (the sentiment, truth, and philosphy of the composition).

None but a lawyer familiar with legal forms and the practice of courts would probably have described so accurately the process of a trial at law. Here is first the cause of difference, described as a "mortal quarrel." The claims of each party are then set forth in argument, the jury properly impanelled, and the verdict properly rendered. This and many passages in the dramas have forced upon biographers and critics a conjecture that Shakespeare at some period of his early life, before going to London, was an attorney's clerk, and while in that employ, was enabled by his remarkable powers to familiarize himself with the most abstruse learning and practice of the English common law. Admitting the possibility that he might have held such a position, any student knows how utterly impossible it would have been for him, without thorough training and practice, to become familiar with the *modus operandi* of courts, and with tenures, reversions, remainders, and titles, which so frequently appear in his dramas, all of which Lord Chancellor Campbell, in his little work of "Shakespeare as a Lawyer," says are correctly used. The truth probably is, that he was never in a law office in his life, except to order a collection suit against some friend who had borrowed a few pounds from him, which he could not pay when due. There is plenty of evidence of that kind, but it was after the plays had been written.

SONNET 47.

Betwixt Mine eye and heart a league is took,
And each doth good turns now unto the other:
When that Mine eye is famish'd for a look,
Or heart in love with sighs himself doth smother,
With My Love's picture then My eye doth feast,
And to the painted banquet bids My heart;
Another time Mine eye is My heart's guest,
And in his thoughts of love doth share a part.
So, either by Thy picture or My Love,
Thyself away art present still with Me;
For Thou not farther than My thoughts canst move,
And I am still with them and they with Thee;
Or, if they sleep, Thy picture in My sight
Awakes My heart to heart's and eye's delight.

The decision of the jury of thoughts in the previous stanza, we are told in this, has effected an arrangement between seeing and feeling, "the eye and the heart," by which they accommodate each other. When he desires to witness the performance of his play, and recalls the beauty of its sentiments, he goes to the theatre, and his "eye doth feast" (and pleased with the performance), "to the painted banquet bids My heart" (his sensibilities are aroused). "Another time Mine eye is My heart's guest" (he is then engaged in composition, in which his reflections are aided by his strong powers of observation). "So either by Thy picture" (by the performance) or "My Love" (my drama), "Thyself" (Thought in delineation) "away art present still with me" (whether at the theatre, or writing at home, Thought, though absent from his sight, is present in his mind). "For Thou not farther than My thoughts can stray," Thou (Truth) never absent from his "thoughts" (his labors), it follows that they are together when he is engaged in writing, and also when the play is being performed. "Or if they sleep" (if he is not at work, and at the theatre), "Thy picture" (the performance) delights his eyes and heart.

Sonnet 48.

How careful was I, when I took My way,
Each trifle under truest bars to thrust,
That to My use it might unused stay
From hands of falsehood, in sure wards of trust!
But Thou, to whom My jewels trifles are,
Most worthy comfort, now My greatest grief,
Thou, best of dearest and Mine only care,
Art left the prey of every vulgar thief.
Thee have I not lock'd up in any chest
Save where Thou art not, though I feel Thou art,

Within the gentle closure of My breast,
From whence at pleasure Thou mayst come and part;
And even thence, Thou wilt be stolen, I fear,
For truth proves thievish for a prize so dear.

Before leaving his lodgings he was careful to secure all trace of his work under lock and key, "truest bars of trust," where no hand could mar or eye see it while he was absent. Meanwhile Thou (Truth) in whom he took "most worthy comfort" (most delight), and who was also "My greatest grief" (his greatest anxiety), "Thou, best of dearest" (best of all his friends), and his "only care," was "left the prey of every vulgar thief" (was free, and exposed to criminal abuse). Thee (Thought) was not "locked up," but the poet carried with him a realizing sense of his presence, feeling that he was with Thou (Truth) "within the gentle closure of his breast," whence he feared, as "truth proves thievish for a prize so dear," he might be influenced by his love for his works to betray their origin himself.

Sonnet 49.

Against that time, if ever that time come,
When I shall see Thee frown on My defects,
Whenas Thy love hath cast his utmost sum,
Call'd to that audit by advis'd respects;
Against that time when Thou shalt strangely pass,
And scarcely greet Me with that sun, Thine eye,
When Love, converted from the thing it was,
Shall reasons find of settled gravity, —

Against that time do I ensconce Me here
Within the knowledge of Mine own desert,
And this My hand against Myself uprear,
To guard the lawful reasons on Thy part:
To leave poor Me Thou hast the strength of laws,
Since why to love, I can allege no cause.

In this stanza he tells in substance the binding force of his obligation to secrecy, as given to Shakespeare. "When I shall see Thee frown on my defects" (if you become dissatisfied with the dramas), "whenas Thy love hath cast his utmost sum" (and decline to share longer with him in the proceeds), "call'd to that audit by advis'd respects" (after a fair trial of their business merits); "when Thou (Truth) shall strangely pass and scarcely greet Me" (when we will, moved by these considerations, abandon the work of composition), "when Love, converted from the thing it was, shall reasons find of settled gravity" (when all intercourse between them is terminated).

"Against that time do I ensconce Me here
Within the knowledge of Mine own desert,
And this My hand against Myself uprear,
To guard the lawful reasons on Thy part."

(He will, proudly conscious of the works and of the injustice awarded them, still protect Shakespeare in all lawful ways from exposure.) Thou (Truth) will have the "strength of laws" to protect him, as there will then be "no cause" for him to remain.

The understanding between Bacon and Shakespeare was doubtless experimental at first. Both probably feared for the success of the drama in theatrical representation. In case of failure, as Shakespeare was to be the avowed author; it was the duty of Bacon to resist any suspicion of the real authorship. It seems from this stanza that Bacon gave a broader meaning to their agreement, and determined in any event, during his own life, to deny all knowledge of the dramas.

SONNET 50.

How heavy do I journey on the way,
When what I seek, My weary travel's end,
Doth teach that ease and that repose to say,
"Thus far the miles are measur'd from Thy Friend!"
The beast that bears Me, tired with My woe,
Plods dully on, to bear that weight in Me,
As if by some instinct the wretch did know
His rider lov'd not speed, being made from Thee:
The bloody spur cannot provoke him on
That sometimes anger thrusts into his hide;
Which heavily he answers with a groan,
More sharp to Me than spurring to his side;
For that same groan doth put this in My mind, —
My grief lies onward and My joy behind.

In this stanza, as well as in one or more preceding it, an apparent desire is manifested by both Bacon and Shakespeare, that the drama he is engaged in writing should be completed with all possible despatch. It is probably for this reason that in a former stanza he regrets that he cannot employ the day as well as the night upon it. The daily demand upon his time is peremptory, and the distance from his lodgings so far as to require a horse for conveyance. This daily journey is "heavy" (tedious and irritating) to him, when he thinks of "what I seek, My weary travel's end" (the work still to be done, before the drama is completed). His daily occupation is one of "ease and repose," from which it may be inferred that he was in daily attendance upon the queen, with little to do, and on the lookout for office. He is constantly worried about the play while absent, and measures the time by the miles of travel he could perform while it continues. "Thus far the miles are measured from Thy Friend" (he is deprived of so much time that he might give to Shakespeare, or in other words, to the drama). His horse, as it seems to him, travels slowly, as if he knew by instinct of his master's wish to remain. He answers the spur with a groan, which reminds the rider that he has a day of dulness and inaction. "My grief lies onward" (which could be so pleasantly and profitably occupied if he could remain at home), "and my joy behind."

SONNET 51.

Thus can My Love excuse the slow offence
Of My dull bearer when from Thee I speed:
From where Thou art why should I haste me thence?
Till I return, of posting is no need.

O, what excuse will My poor beast then find,
When swift extremity can seem but slow?
Then should I spur, though mounted on the wind;
In winged speed no motion shall I know:
Then can no horse with My desire keep pace;
Therefore desire, of perfect'st love being made,
Shall neigh — no dull flesh — in his fiery race;
But Love, for Love, thus shall excuse My jade:
Since from Thee going he went wilful-slow,
Towards Thee I'll run, and give him leave to go.

The return from his day's absence is described in this stanza. He apologizes to "My Love" (the drama) for the laziness of his horse when going away from her and Thou. "For where Thou art why should I haste me thence?" as if he had said it would be strange indeed if he left "Thou" and "My Love," his two dearest friends, except he was compelled. "Till I return, of posting is no need" (until the day's occupation was over, he need be in no hurry). But when that hour arrives, he will have no excuse to offer for a tardy return. "When swift extremity can seem but slow" (when the extremest speed will not equal that of his eagerness to complete the journey). If he was mounted on the wind he would spur it into "winged speed," and experience "no motion" in the transit if he obeyed his desire. No horse could pace with his desire. But as his desire is made of perfect love, and not "dull flesh," it shall answer to "My Love," as a horse would reply with a "neigh" to his mate. This will be sufficient explanation for his dulness when away, and the speed of his return.

SONNET 52.

So am I as the rich, whose blessed key
Can bring him to his sweet up-locked treasure,
The which he will not every hour survey,
For blunting the fine point of seldom pleasure.
Therefore are feasts so solemn and so rare,
Since, seldom coming, in the long year set,
Like stones of worth they thinly placed are,
Or captain jewels in the carcanet.
So is the time that keeps You as My chest,
Or as the wardrobe which the robe doth hide,
To make some special instant special blest,
By new unfolding his imprison'd pride.
  Blessed are You, whose worthiness gives scope,
  Being had, to triumph, being lack'd, to hope.

He explains in this stanza the peculiar pleasure he feels on his return to his work. As a rich man derives more happiness from an occasional survey of the wealth, which he keeps secured by lock and key, so he is more sensible to the pleasure derived from working on his drama at intervals, than he would be if constantly employed. Feasts are more highly appreciated than they would be if of more frequent occurrence. As the attractiveness of precious jewels is increased when they are separate in setting, so the time which conceals You (Beauty) adds to your fascinations as often as you are exposed to view. As the wardrobe which contains the robe unfolded on great occasions, so You (Beauty) unfold new delights to every moment he devotes to your service. All succeed who have you, and all hope who have you not.

Sonnet 53.

What is Your substance, whereof are You made,
That millions of strange shadows on You tend?
Since every one hath, every one, one shade,
And You, but one, can every shadow lend.
Describe Adonis, and the counterfeit
Is poorly imitated after You;
On Helen's cheek all art of beauty set,
And You in Grecian tires are painted new:
Speak of the spring and foison of the year,
The one doth shadow of Your beauty show,
The other as Your bounty doth appear;
And You in every blessed shape we know.
In all external grace You have some part,
But You like none, none You, for constant heart.

The power of You (Beauty) is described in this stanza. In view of the countless forms which Beauty assumes, he is eager to learn the elements of which he is composed. "What is Your substance, whereof are You made?" Every person has but one shadow, but you, who are but one, can "lend" (create) millions. All attempts to imitate your description of Adonis are failures. The time of writing the poem of "Venus and Adonis" could not be better suited to that particular period he all along has described as being employed upon the dramas. It was among the first of his efforts. "The True Tragedy," "History of the Contention," "Two Gentlemen of Verona," and "Taming the Shrew" had appeared before it was published, but Shakespeare first appeared as the author of "Venus and Adonis." The following is the description of Adonis referred to:—

"Thrice fairer than myself," thus she began,
"The field's chief flower, sweet above compare,
Stain to all nymphs, more lovely than a man,
More white and red than doves and roses are,
Nature that made thee, with herself at strife,
Saith that the world hath ending with thy life."

Venus and Adonis, Stanza 2.

"On Helen's cheek, all art of beauty set." This line has reference to the beauty of Helen as depicted in various passages in the play of "Troilus and Cressida," which, though not published until 1609, was probably fresh in his memory at the time this stanza was prepared. "And you in Grecian tires are painted new," probably has allusion to other characters in the same play, and to the plays "Timon of Athens" and "A Midsummer Night's Dream." Spring reflects Beauty in its verdure and freshness, and "the foison of the year" (autumn) in its abundance. There is nothing attractive, and no "external grace" of which Beauty is not a part. But it is evanescent of itself. (It is only when it lends itself to something that it is of any use. It is inconstant, fleeting, impalpable.) "You like none, none You, for constant heart."

Sonnet 54.

O, how much more doth beauty beauteous seem
By that sweet ornament which truth doth give!
The rose looks fair, but fairer we it deem
For that sweet odour which doth in it live.
The canker-blooms have full as deep a dye,
As the perfumed tincture of the roses,

Hang on such thorns, and play as wantonly,
When summer's breath their masked buds discloses.
But, for their virtue only is their show,
They live unwoo'd, and unrespected fade,
Die to themselves. Sweet roses do not so;
Of their sweet deaths are sweetest odours made:
  And so of You, beauteous and lovely youth,
  When that shall vade, my verse distills Your truth.

The adornment which Truth gives to Beauty is described in this stanza. Fair as the rose is in appearance, it is equally prized for its perfume. The canker is as rich in hue and as graceful in appearance as the rose, but wanting in perfume, it fades and dies neglected and unnoticed. But the sweetest odors are made by the "death" (the faded leaves) of the rose. So of Beauty, which alone dies to itself, but when used in the illustration of Truth, as it is in "my verse" (this poem), the truth it adorns, like the perfume of the rose, will give it permanent existence.

Sonnet 55.

Not marble, nor the gilded monuments
Of princes, shall outlive this powerful rhyme;
But You shall shine more bright in these contents
Than unswept stone, besmear'd with sluttish time.
When wasteful war shall statues overturn,
And broils root out the work of masonry,
Nor Mars his sword nor war's quick fire shall burn
The living record of Your memory.
'Gainst death and all-oblivious enmity
Shall You pace forth; Your praise shall still find room

Even in the eyes of all posterity
That wear this world out to the ending doom.
So, till the judgment that Yourself arise,
You live in this, and dwell in lovers' eyes.

In this stanza the duration of Beauty's life, harmoniously united with Truth in this poem, is portrayed. It shall outlive all material creation,—the "marble" and "gilded monuments of princes," and the fabrics of stone which time has covered with mosses and discolorations. The ravage and devastation of war, which destroys statues, razes the most solid structures, and burns towns, shall not destroy "the living record of Your memory" (this poem, in which is recorded the history of the dramas). You shall survive all who live; even oblivion has no power to hide you. "All posterity" shall see and delight in you to "the ending doom" (forever). You shall live in "this" poem (this poem in its history will give you life in the dramas), where you will "dwell in lovers' eyes" (delighting all who see you displayed in them).

Sonnet 56.

Sweet love, renew Thy force; be it not said
Thy edge should blunter be than appetite,
Which but to-day by feeding is allay'd,
To-morrow sharpen'd in his former might:
So, love, be Thou; although to-day Thou fill
Thy hungry eyes, even till they wink with fulness,
To-morrow see again, and do not kill
The spirit of love with a perpetual dulness,

> Let this sad interim like the ocean be
> Which parts the shore, where two contracted new
> Come daily to the banks, that, when they see
> Return of love, more blest may be the view;
> Else call it winter, which being full of care
> Makes summer's welcome thrice more wish'd, more rare.

Bacon must have been greatly enamored with his writings to promise for them, even at this early stage, when but four of the dramas had been written, such unending life. In this stanza the meaning insinuates that a suspension of work upon the dramas is likely to occur, but that after a time it will be resumed. Meantime he is anxious that his love for the work should suffer no abatement. Like the appetite, satiated "to-day" (with present labor) with like or greater eagerness, may his hunger for resuming work return to-morrow, so that "the spirit of love" (the power of delineation) may not forsake him. Like two lovers, who, separated by the ocean, their vows just plighted, go daily to the shores by agreement to meditate upon their affection for each other, so let the "sad interim" (the period of this suspension) keep the subject of future composition constantly in mind, that on "return of love, more blest may be the view" (he may exceed his former efforts). Or let the intermission be like winter with its coldness, which makes summer's warmth and beauty welcome and delightful. It will be seen hereafter that winter and summer are used to symbolize the very conditions which are here suggested by them.

SONNET 57.

Being your slave, what should I do but tend
Upon the hours and times of Your desire?
I have no precious time at all to spend,
Nor services to do, till You require.
Nor dare I chide the world-without-end hour
Whilst I, My sovereign, watch the clock for You,
Nor think the bitterness of absence sour
When You have bid Your servant once adieu;
Nor dare I question with My jealous thought
Where You may be, or Your affairs suppose,
But, like a sad slave, stay and think of nought
Save, where You are, how happy You make those.
So true a fool is love that in Your will,
Though You do anything, he thinks no ill.

This stanza and the following one are addressed to Queen Elizabeth. The following extract is taken from the first volume of the Biographia Brittanica, page 373:—

"After discharging the office of reader at Gray's Inn, which he [Bacon] did, in 1588, when in the twenty-sixth year of his age, he was become so considerable, that the queen, who never over-valued any man's abilities, thought fit to call him to her service in a way which did him very great honor, by appointing him her counsel learned in the law extraordinary; by which, though she contributed abundantly to his reputation, yet she added but very little to his fortune; and indeed, in this respect he was never very much indebted to her majesty, how much soever he might be in all others."

This appointment, which obliged him to be in daily attendance upon her majesty, was probably the cause of his absence from his quarters at Gray's Inn, during the business hours of every day, while the office continued. It made him, as he says in the stanza, the "slave" of the queen. In the discharge of its duties he was bound to "tend upon the hours and times of her desire" (to obey her pleasure, however exacting). This gave him "no precious time at all to spend" (no time that he could devote to the composition of his dramas), "nor services to do till you require" (nor any other service except under her special direction). As a consequence, his time was for the most part unoccupied, but necessarily spent in waiting the queen's orders. He meantime dared not "chide the world-without-end hour, whilst I, my sovereign, watch the clock for you" (how heavy soever the hours might pass with him, his fear of the queen's anger prevented him from complaining). He did not even "think the bitterness of absence sour, when you have bid your servant once adieu" (he could not complain, when she left him to await her return, of her absence, so unprofitably spent by him). "Nor dare I question with my jealous thought where you may be, or your affairs suppose" (he dared not even to inquire into the occasion of her absence). "But, like a sad slave, stay and think of nought save, where you are, how happy you make those" (but he must await her return in a state of complete passivity, except as occasion might offer for some delicate flattery, or pleasant allusion to her own powers of fascination while absent). This service made his loyalty ridiculous, and obliged him to praise in the same strain both the vices and virtues of the queen.

No historian has ever drawn with truer pen the predominant characteristics of Elizabeth than Bacon in this stanza. Proud, capricious, despotic, high-tempered, selfish, suspicious, and overbearing, she exacted the entire submission of every one she honored, and filled the very atmosphere of her court with fear. Bacon's life at court at this time was monotonous, unoccupied, and insecure, but the hope of preferment — an ambition to shine as a great statesman and great lawyer — rendered it endurable. For this hope, ever uppermost in his thoughts, he submitted to all the "whips and spurs" of fortune, while inwardly worshipping all that was true and beautiful in nature and character. He was truly great as a philosopher and poet, but cringing and submissive as a courtier and statesman. His wonderful abilities made his faults the more conspicuous. Similar failings in some of his famous contemporaries have escaped the criticism which has so sharply assailed his memory. It had been fortunate for him and the world if his life had been devoted to those pursuits only for which, as he says when speaking of his public career, "it was better fitted."

SONNET 58.

That god forbid that made Me first Your slave,
I should in thought control Your times of pleasure,
Or at Your hand the account of hours to crave,
Being Your vassal, bound to stay Your leisure!
O, let Me suffer, being at Your beck,
The imprison'd absence of Your liberty;
And patience, tame to sufferance, bide each check,
Without accusing You of injury.
Be where You list, Your charter is so strong
That You Yourself may privilege Your time
To what You will; to You it doth belong
Yourself to pardon of self-doing crime.
I am to wait, though waiting so be hell;
Not blame Your pleasure, be it ill or well.

In this stanza he accepts submissively all the humiliation and abasement to which he is subjected as an attendant at court. "That god forbid that made me first your slave" (that ambition that causes him to look to the queen for preferment), that he should fail to accommodate his time to suit hers. He is her "vassal," and bound to stay at court until she can see him, though it is like a prison to him. If he feels impatient, he still must submit to suffer, — bear with all delays, from whatever cause, without complaint against her. She must occupy her time as she pleases, as it is entirely under her control, — is her right, — and she need not respect his wishes at all, as she has power to pardon herself for any wrong she may do. And though the waiting, which absents him from work upon his dramas, "be hell" to him, he can find no fault with his queen, whether he is delayed with or without cause. In both these stanzas the key of "You," which impersonates Beauty, is necessarily used in substitution for the queen, for the reason, probably, that it was indispensable. By reading the stanzas as if applied to Beauty, the key is perfect, and I was disposed to confine it to that meaning; but its perfect adaptability to the appointment he received, and the sequent meaning it gives to the probable suspension in his writing, foreshadowed in the fifty-sixth stanza, as well as the absence daily imposed on him, which he so laments, has confirmed my belief that he intended to address the queen, and also preserve the key, by making the stanza equally applicable to Beauty.

SONNET 59.

If there be nothing new, but that which is
Hath been before, how are our brains beguil'd,
Which, laboring for invention, bear amiss
The second burthen of a former child!
O, that record could, with a backward look,
Even of five hundred courses of the sun,
Show Me Your image in some antique book,
Since mind at first in character was done!
That I might see what the old world could say
To this composed wonder of your frame;
Whether we 're mended, or whether better they,
Or whether revolution be the same.
O, sure I am, the wits of former days
To subjects worse have given admiring praise.

Comparison between the stories upon which his plays are founded and the plays themselves is made in this stanza. If these plays are not new in their new dress, he has spent his time unprofitably in "laboring for invention" to make them so. Of their comparative merits, he would like to have the opinion of the "old world" (the people who lived five hundred years before his time), when the stories upon which his dramas were founded were written; in the days of Cinthio, Saxo Grammaticus, and other writers, when "mind at first in character was done" (when the first modern attempts at story-telling were made), and hear what their opinion would be "of this composed wonder of your frame" (of the reproduction he has made of their works), whether they are improved or not, or "whether revolution be the same" (whether the world has remained stationary, without advancement). He ventures the assertion that the "wits" (the critics, authors, and readers) of those times had been pleased and satisfied with works less deserving than those he has written.

SONNET 60.

Like as the waves make towards the pebbled shore,
So do our minutes hasten to their end;
Each changing place with that which goes before,
In sequent toil all forwards do contend.
Nativity, once in the main of light,
Crawls to maturity, wherewith being crown'd,
Crooked eclipses 'gainst his glory fight,
And Time that gave doth now his gift confound.
Time doth transfix the flourish set on youth
And delves the parallels in Beauty's brow,

> Feeds on the rarities of nature's truth,
> And nothing stands but for his scythe to mow;
> And yet to times in hope my verse shall stand,
> Praising Thy worth, despite his cruel hand.

This stanza is a reflex of the advancement of growth and life from infancy to maturity. The minutes are compared to the waves in their approach to the beach, each changing place with the one before it, and all eager in its march to reach the limit of its bounds. "Nativity, once in the main of light" (the infant just born), "crawls to maturity" (feels the time as long until he reaches manhood), "wherewith being crown'd, crooked eclipses 'gainst his glory fight" (when attained, he meets with worldly troubles which darken the bright path he had marked for himself in early years). "And Time that gave doth now his gift confound" (if he has been favored by education, or wealth, the world is full of obstacles to the success in life he had anticipated). "Time doth transfix the flourish set on youth" (the promises and flatteries which accompanied his youth, and taught him to believe he was destined for great achievements, find no fruition among the disappointments and cares that assail him in his struggle with the world). "And delves the parallels in Beauty's brow" (wrinkles him with sorrow, regret, and anguish). "Feeds on the vanities of nature's truth" (it is wasted in the follies and vices of the world). "And nothing stands but for his scythe to mow" (hopes are blasted, life is overcast, and no prospect of worldly attainment or promotion before him).

This I conceive to have been written as expressive of Bacon's own disappointment in early life. No young man of that age was favored with better opportunities, and none ever blessed with greater abilities and aptitudes of thought and desire to profit by them. The death of his father, want of fortune, and force of circumstances, which deprived him of congenial studies and occupations, clouded his early manhood, made him a dependent, and changed the whole course of his life. It is quite probable, however, but for these changes, the world never would have been blessed with his immortal dramas.

This stanza is also suggestive of the thoughts contained in the celebrated speech of Jaques in "As You Like It," commencing "All the world's a stage," etc., and may have been written in allusion to that play.

Sonnet 61.

Is it Thy will Thy image should keep open
My heavy eyelids to the weary night?
Dost Thou desire My slumbers should be broken,
While shadows like to Thee do mock My sight?
Is it Thy spirit that Thou send'st from Thee
So far from home into My deeds to pry,
To find out shames and idle hours in Me,
The scope and tenor of Thy jealousy?
O, no! Thy Love, though much, is not so great:
It is My Love that keeps Mine eye awake;

> Mine own *true* Love that doth My rest defeat,
> To play the watchman ever for Thy sake:
> For Thee watch I, whilst Thou dost wake elsewhere,
> From Me far off, with others all too near.

He tells in this stanza that Shakespeare, though present to his thoughts, is not the principal motive which impels him to work upon his dramas. "Is it Thy will Thy image should keep open My heavy eyelids to the weary night?" (am I influenced by the thought of Will Shakespeare in the drama I am writing?) "Dost Thou [Truth] desire my slumbers should be broken, while shadows like to Thee [Shakespeare] do mock my sight?" (shall I stop writing, or lose sleep on your account?) "Is it Thy [Shakespeare's] spirit that Thou [Truth] send'st from Thee [Thought] so far from home into My deeds to pry?" (does my night work on the drama require your presence for any purpose?) "To find out shame and idle hours in Me, the scope and tenor of Thy jealousy?" (can you tell whether my writings are ill or well, or whether they should be completed sooner or later?) "O, no! Thy Love, though much, is not so great" (your interest, though valuable, is of another kind, and not equal to any of these services). "It is My Love [my drama] that keeps Mine eye awake, Mine own *true* Love that doth My rest defeat" (it is my drama, which is "My own true Love," that influences me to work, and also to be watchful of you, Shakespeare). I watch for you when "Thou dost wake elsewhere" (when Truth is elsewhere, and I am not busy with my writing). "From Me far off, with others all too near" (and liable to be employed by others in their writings). This stanza virtually denies to Shakespeare any work in the composition of the dramas.

SONNET 62.

Sin of self-love possesseth all Mine eye
And all My soul and all My every part;
And for this sin there is no remedy,
It is so grounded inward in My heart.
Methinks no face so gracious is as Mine,
No shape so true, no truth of such account;
And for Myself Mine own worth do define,
As I all other in all worths surmount.
But when My glass shows Me Myself indeed,
Bated and chopp'd with tann'd antiquity,
Mine own self-love quite contrary I read;
Self so self-loving were iniquity.
'T is Thee, Myself, that for Myself I praise,
Painting My age with beauty of Thy days.

He apologizes in this stanza for the self-love he has exhibited in the previous stanza by claiming for himself the merit of composing the dramas. Self-love possesses him "in all my every part." Its control of him is so entire that there is "no remedy" for it. Under its influence he thinks no one handsomer than he is, so well shaped, so perfect in character. In his own estimation he excels "all others." But when he sees himself in his reflections "bated and chopp'd with tann'd antiquity" (worn and thin from his studies and closet exercises, and a life of seclusion), he is undeceived and reminded of the folly of such self-love. It is all for "Thee, Myself" (my thoughts in delineation), that "for Myself I praise, painting My age with beauty of Thy days" (bestowing his thoughts upon the times in which he happens to live).

Sonnet 63.

Against My Love shall be, as I am now,
With Time's injurious hand crush'd and o'erworn,
When hours have drain'd his blood, and fill'd his brow
With lines and wrinkles, when his youthful morn
Hath travell'd on to age's steepy night,
And all those beauties whereof now he 's king
Are vanishing or vanish'd out of sight,
Stealing away the treasure of his spring, —
For such a time do I now fortify
Against confounding age's cruel knife,
That he shall never cut from memory
My sweet Love's beauty, though My lover's life;
His beauty shall in these black lines be seen, —
And they shall live, and he in them still green.

In this stanza he declares that he writes this poem to perpetuate the dramas. "Against My Love [it will be remembered that Shakespeare was added to "My Love," but not as a *true* love, in the fortieth stanza] shall be, as I am now" (the time will come when Shakespeare will be enfeebled as he is). Time will wear out his vigor, attenuate and weaken his frame. His blood will be thinned, and wrinkles and lines will mark his visage.

His morn of youth will be superseded by the night of infirm old age. His freshness and joyousness, now so attractive, and all the strength of his manhood, will disappear, carrying with them the hopes and aspirations of his early life, and the ambition and energy of his spring. "Against confounding age's cruel knife" (to forestall the effect of these infirmities in Shakespeare), and that they may not be equally destructive to "My sweet Love's beauty" (his dramas), though they will destroy "My lover's [Shakespeare's] life," "these black lines" (the printed lines composing this poem), shall preserve them, and their beauty shall "in them still be green" (always fresh).

May it not have been possible that it was one part of the arrangement between Bacon and Shakespeare, that Shakespeare should abandon all care for the dramas at the time of his retirement from the theatre, and that their history from that period should be left for the world to solve? There is something very curious about the closing period of Shakespeare's life. No evidence has ever been found to show that he bestowed any attention upon the plays after they ceased to add to his revenues. Nothing in his will shows that he claimed any property in them at the time of his death. His effects and papers did not contain any reference to them, nor was there even a letter or manuscript from which it could be inferred that he had ever written a line of them. He died and left no other sign than the fearful lines on his tomb which have so long prevented the removal of his bones to Westminster Abbey. Either Bacon knew at the time he wrote this stanza that this was to be the condition of the dramas at Shakespeare's death, or that Shakespeare was not likely from habit or inclination to care for their preservation. I incline to the former opinion, as well because of the intense interest manifested for their perpetuity in this poem, as the words in Bacon's will bequeathing his works and memory to "the next ages and foreign countries." He foresaw the time when the authorship of these works would be investigated, and "for such a time" did he "fortify" against the "confounding" which "cruel age" would be likely to introduce. That "confounding" has come, and the question will not rest without a just settlement.

SONNET 64.

When I have seen by Time's fell hand defac'd,
The rich proud cost of outworn buried age,
When sometime lofty towers I see down-raz'd,
And brass eternal slave to mortal rage,
When I have seen the hungry ocean gain
Advantage on the kingdom of the shore,
And the firm soil win of the watery main,
Increasing store with loss and loss with store, —
When I have seen such interchange of state,
Or state itself confounded to decay,

Ruin hath taught Me thus to ruminate,
That Time will come and take My Love away.
This thought is as a death, which cannot choose
But weep to have that which it fears to lose.

He assigns other reasons in this stanza for his fears concerning the perpetuity of the dramas. The devastations wrought by Time upon the richest and most sacred memorials, the overthrow of "lofty towers," and the destruction of works and statues of brass, in broils and insurrections; the encroachments of the sea upon the land, and the gains of the land from the sea;—all these interchanges, as well as the changes in governments often ending in ruin, have caused him to fear that a like calamity may occur to his Love (his dramas). He is overwhelmed with regret at the thought, "which cannot choose but weep to have that which it fears to lose" (and grieves that he cannot claim the dramas as his own, since he is so much concerned for their future condition).

This stanza corroborates my impression that there must have been some understanding by which the dramas were to be abandoned by both Bacon and Shakespeare, and no further explanation of them given than such as appeared attributing them to Shakespeare, and their concealed history in this poem. This poem was probably understood by Shakespeare, at the time it was written, to contain a full history of the dramas. If so, it goes far to account for the meagre evidence concerning their origin. Bacon gave to time the revealment of a history which he dared not tell during his life. Shakespeare retired to enjoy the fortune he had acquired, and the fame of his imputed authorship, until the true author should be discovered. I have no doubt that Bacon reasoned that there was fame enough for him in the Novum Organum, De Augmentis, and his other philosophical works; but at the same time felt a deep pang of regret whenever it occurred to him that these great dramas might never be appreciated as the first and richest fruits of his mighty genius.

SONNET 65.

Since brass, nor stone, nor earth, nor boundless sea,
But sad mortality o'ersways their power,
How with this rage shall beauty hold a plea,
Whose action is no stronger than a flower?
O, how shall summer's honey breath hold out
Against the wrackful siege of battering days,
When rocks impregnable are not so stout,
Nor gates of steel so strong, but time decays?
O fearful meditation! where, alack,
Shall Time's best jewel from Time's chest lie hid?
Or what strong hand can hold his swift foot back?
Or who his spoil of Beauty can forbid?
O, none, unless this miracle have might,
That in black ink My Love may still shine bright.

He infers from the argument in the preceding stanza that nothing can preserve his dramas, unless it is the ink with which from time to time they may be printed. All durable objects of human origin are sooner or later destroyed by the ravages of Time,—even the sea and earth are subject to changes wrought by him. How, with no adequate power of resistance, is Beauty to contend successfully with this destroyer? Amid the wrecks which war and siege make, what shall prolong her sweet life? How can she live when Time consumes the strongest structures of stone and metal? It is fearful to contemplate what may become of "Time's best jewel," or where she may be concealed to escape this general ruin. There is no help for her unless the "miracle" (the marvellous power) of being multiplied in printer's ink shall cause "My Love" (the dramas), to "shine bright" (to be perpetuated).

SONNET 66.

Tir'd with all these, for restful death I cry,—
As, to behold desert a beggar born,
And needy nothing trimm'd in jollity,
And purest faith unhappily foresworn,
And gilded honour shamefully misplac'd,
And maiden virtue rudely strumpeted,
And right perfection wrongfully disgrac'd,
And strength by limping sway disabled,
And art made tongue-tied by authority,
And folly, doctor-like, controlling skill,
And simple truth miscall'd simplicity,
And captive good attending captain ill;
Tir'd with all these, from these would I begone,
Save that, to die, I leave My Love alone.

His object in this stanza, in summarizing the subjects illustrated by the plays written and performed, at this time, is doubtless to show that by their departure from Truth and nature they were evil and corrupt in their influence. He had no patience with their character, and when he says, "for restful death I cry," it was a polite form of expressing our slang phrase "give us a rest," and meant the same. The playwrights were crowding the stage with sensational pieces, not unlike those of our own day. The subjects as expressed in the stanza explain themselves better than any language of mine can do it. They show that the theatre in Elizabeth's time was not reliable as a school of morality, and the taste which tolerated the grand creations of Bacon was better satisfied, perhaps, with the blood-curdling dramas of Webster, or the licentious comedies of Green, Ben Jonson, and Beaumont and Fletcher. Whatever the plays, and whoever the writers, no stronger evidence of their immoral tendencies are needed than that they were condemned by the author of the plays attributed to Shakespeare. His distaste for them was strong enough to make him wish to "begone" from them, "save that to die" (to go from them) would be to "leave My Love alone" (to forsake his own dramas).

Sonnet 67.

Ah! wherefore with infection should he live,
And with his presence grace impiety,
That sin by him advantage should achieve
And lace itself with his society?

Why should false painting imitate his cheek,
And steal dead seeing of his living hue?
Why should poor beauty indirectly seek
Roses of shadow, since his rose is true?
Why should he live, now Nature bankrupt is,
Beggar'd of blood to blush through lively veins?
For she hath no exchequer now but his,
And, proud of many, lives upon his gains.
O, him she stores, to show what wealth she had
In days long since, before these last so bad.

His contempt for the dramas of his own day, emphasized by his regret at seeing his own dramas in their company, is more fully expressed in this and the following stanza. Why should the beauty which he has illustrated live with such "infection" (exposed to the contamination of their influence), and thus in representation tolerate their untruth and vulgarity? Why should their profanity and obscenity find a place on the stage where his dramas are performed? Why should those who personate their characters imitate the natural beauty of the characters he had drawn, by giving a false color to their faces, and a livid hue to their flesh? Why should Beauty as exhibited by them, by these and other indirect means, decorate himself, when his own adornment only is the truest of ornaments? Why should Beauty, devoid of all natural grace, "beggar'd of blood to blush through lively veins" (his true nature concealed with paint and gewgaws), be attempted in the performances? Nature "hath no exchequer now but his" (he in his truth furnishes the real wealth of all true characterizations), and "proud of many, lives upon his gäins" (many dramas have been written in which life has been fitly represented), but they are withdrawn from the stage. Their great superiority to those now in vogue is painfully apparent by contrast.

SONNET 68.

Thus in his cheek the map of days outworn,
When beauty liv'd and died as flowers do now,
Before these bastard signs of fair were born,
Or durst inhabit on a living brow;
Before the golden tresses of the dead,
The right of sepulchres, were shorn away,
To live a second life on second head,
Ere Beauty's dead fleece made another gay:
In him those holy antique hours are seen,
Without all ornament, itself and true,
Making no summer of another's green,
Robbing no old to dress his Beauty new;
And him as for a map doth Nature store,
To show false Art what beauty was of yore.

His indignation at the artificiality in which the drama is represented is expressed in this stanza. "Thus is his cheek the map of days outworn, when beauty liv'd and died as flowers do now" (we see, as upon a map, in the drama of past years, what Beauty was when life and death in character were naturally represented). "Before these bastard signs of fair were born" (before personal decoration was introduced, or even permitted in use; before the hair was cut from the heads of the dead to adorn the heads of the living, thus using the ornaments which gave Beauty to the grave, to give life to a false show of gayety. "In him those holy antique hours are seen, without all ornament, itself and true" (a time when any adornment of natural beauty would have been to profane it; it was most beautiful as nature made it). In the words of Thomson:—

> "Beauty when unadorn'd 's adorn'd the most."

It "made no summer of another's green" (did not imitate in one performance what properly belonged to another); "robbing no old to dress his Beauty new" (nor steal the sentiment from one author to supply the deficiencies of another). The falsities of art of which he complains will appear on comparison with the representations of former days.

His own dramas, doubtless performed with all the appliances so hateful to him, were what rendered them so specially obnoxious. His dramas were all sufficient of themselves to illustrate the truth they contained, and all outside paraphernalia, while it did not improve the sentiments they contained, imparted a false glare to the moral and natural beauty in which truth was enveloped. Of themselves, they were the very embodiment of truth, clothed in the beauty of sentiment and poetry. What could painting and false hair, and the other gewgaws used in theatrical display, add to them? He was disgusted with these appliances.

His whole soul rejected them; but there was no remedy, and he dismisses the subject by showing in contrast how far they were surpassed in the early days of the drama, before such adornments were brought into use.

Sonnet 69.

Those parts of Thee that the world's eye doth view
Want nothing that the thought of hearts can mend;
All tongues, the voice of souls, give Thee that due,
Uttering bare truth, even so as foes commend.
Thy outward thus with outward praise is crown'd;
But those same tongues that give Thee so Thine own,
In other accents do this praise confound,
By seeing farther than the eye hath shown.
They look into the beauty of Thy mind,
And that, in guess, they measure by Thy deeds;
Then, churls, their thoughts, although their eyes were kind,
To Thy fair flower add the rank smell of weeds:
  But why Thy odour matcheth not Thy show,
  The solve is this, that Thou dost common grow.

He tells in this stanza of the reception accorded to his plays by the public. "Those parts of Thee that the world's eye doth view" (the impression which in performance they make upon the audience), "want nothing that the thought of hearts can mend" (need no addition in sentiment, thought, or action); "all tongues" (the voice of souls) "give Thee that due" (this is the opinion of all who can appreciate them). "Even so as foes commend" (probably this refers to other playwriters who were jealous of Shakespeare's success as an author). "Thine outward thus with outward praise is crown'd" (in external representation they are abundantly successful). "But those same tongues that give Thee so Thine own" (the same audiences, thus lavish of praise of their scenic display and the characters), "in other accents do this praise confound, by seeing farther than the eye hath shown" (their criticisms of the subject-matter of the play are so various and conflicting as to "confound" or perplex them in forming any settled opinion of its merits). "They look into the beauty of Thy mind, and that, in guess, they measure by Thy deeds" (they disagree about the design of the author, and the truth he intended to illustrate, and not fully comprehending it, guess at such conclusions as the action of the play would seem to warrant). In this manner, though pleased, they mistake the "fair flowers" (the real beauty), and "add the rank smell of weeds" (attribute meanings to it that are incorrect). "But why Thy odour matcheth not Thy show, the solve is this, that Thou dost common grow" (the reason why the plays are not appreciated at their true worth is because other writers having witnessed them are now introducing plays in which they aim to illustrate truth, and this makes Thou (Truth) so common, that in his dramas he is lost sight of).

SONNET 70.

That Thou art blam'd shall not be Thy defect,
For slander's mark was ever yet the fair;

The ornament of beauty is Suspect,
A crow that flies in heaven's sweetest air.
So Thou be good, slander doth but approve
Thy worth the greater, being woo'd of time;
For canker vice the sweetest buds doth love,
And Thou present'st a pure unstained prime.
Thou hast pass'd by the ambush of young days,
Either not assail'd or victor being charg'd;
Yet this Thy praise cannot be so Thy praise,
To tie up envy evermore enlarg'd;
If some suspect of ill mask'd not Thy show,
Then Thou alone kingdoms of hearts shouldst owe.

He declares in this stanza that it is for no lack of merit in his dramas that the public does not fully appreciate them. There is no defect in their thought or truth, but being praised and admired, it is but natural that they should be a mark for slander and suspicion. Those who add ornament and decoration to beauty are the first to find fault with those who are content to let beauty speak for herself without these additions. If Thou (Truth) is preserved in purity, slander helps instead of hurts thought, and Time, which discovers and exposes his malice, adds thereby to the worth and might of thought. Thou's purity assailed by slander is like the canker which assails the sweetest flowers. But what has Thou to fear from it? In his youthful days (when first brought in contact with inexperience) he escaped assault, or when assailed, always proved victorious. Even these successes cannot silence envy, which is always free and ready to do its work. If he escaped altogether, he would be the only one in the world who was worshipped by all.

SONNET 71.

No longer mourn for Me when I am dead,
Than you shall hear the surly sullen bell
Give warning to the world that I am fled
From this vile world, with vilest worms to dwell;
Nay, if You read this line, remember not
The hand that writ it, for I love You so,
That I in Your sweet thoughts would be forgot,
If thinking on Me then should make You woe.
O, if, I say, You look upon this verse
When I perhaps compounded am with clay,
Do not so much as My poor name rehearse,
But let Your love even with My life decay,
  Lest the wise world should look into Your moan,
  And mock You with me after I am gone.

This refers to that period in the life of Bacon (1594) when by a vacancy in the office of solicitor-general he was encouraged to apply for the appointment. "He had been counsel extraordinary to the queen," says Chambers, "since 1590, and three years afterwards sat in Parliament for the county of Middlesex." Essex, at that time in the plenitude of his power, the special favorite of Elizabeth, was Bacon's most ardent supporter. He spared neither pains nor means to obtain his appointment. Bacon regarded it as a certainty, and as the duties of the office would require his constant and unceasing labor, he felt that the time had come when he must abandon play-writing, and bid farewell to literary pursuits.

In anticipation of this change, his anxieties were increased, lest the queen should discover that he had written for the theatre and reject him. These stanzas undoubtedly reflect the condition of his mind at that time. The death of which he speaks is the abandonment of writing which he contemplates. The stanzas are addressed to You (Beauty). "No longer mourn for Me when I am dead, than You shall hear the surly sullen bell" (let me be forgotten as the writer of these beautiful dramas as soon as my appointment is announced). "Give warning to the world that I am fled" (gone from my lodgings) "from this vile world" (from Gray's Inn), "with vilest worms to dwell" (to the criminal courts of Westminster). "Nay, if You read this line, remember not the hand that writ it" (no beauty in the sentiment or style of the composition must betray him), "for I love You so, that I in Your sweet thoughts would be forgot" (he would not wish to be known as the writer). "If thinking on me then should make You woe" (as it would cause his ruin). "O, if, I say, You look upon this verse when I perhaps compounded am with clay" (when he is really dead), "do not so much as My poor name rehearse, but let Your love even with My life decay" (even then his name must not be known). "Lest the wise world should look into Your moan, and mock You with me after I am gone" (lest the world, recognizing him as the writer, should visit with contempt and ridicule the one in whose name he wrote).

SONNET 72.

O, lest the world should task You to recite
What merit liv'd in Me, that You should love
After My death, dear love, forget Me quite,
For You in Me can nothing worthy prove;
Unless You would devise some virtuous lie,
To do more for Me than Mine own desert,
And hang more praise upon deceased I
Than niggard Truth would willingly impart:
O, lest Your true love may seem false in this,
That You for love speak well of Me untrue,
My name be buried where My body is,
And live no more to shame nor Me nor You!
For I am sham'd by that which I bring forth,
And so should You, to love things nothing worth.

In this stanza he urges his own unworthiness as a reason for the concealment of his name as author of the dramas. "O, lest the world should task You to recite what merit liv'd in Me" (lest it should be suspected that he had written the dramas), "that You [Beauty] should love" (and they should be criticised, to discover, if possible, his style), "after My death, dear love, forget Me quite" (after his appointment, let no mention of him lead to his betrayal), "unless You would devise some virtuous lie, to do more for Me than Mine own desert" (unless you can divert suspicion by inventing a story more probable and easier of belief than any doubts), "and hang more praise upon deceased I than niggard Truth would willingly impart" (and by speaking well of him, in flattering terms, render his position an honor to him, instead of a grief). "O, lest Your true love" (your beauty as delineated in the dramas) "may seem false in this, that You for love speak well of Me untrue" (may be belied by bestowing praise on him by a skilfully contrived falsehood to conceal his own untruth). "My name be buried where My body is" (only mentioned in connection with his public position), "and live no more to shame nor Me nor You" (and no longer be known as a writer for the stage, as a bencher at Gray's Inn, or as a dabbler with the muses). "For I am sham'd by that which I bring forth" (it was a shame to him that his dramas should be presented in the theatre, before miscellaneous audiences, which could not appreciate them), and you will be equally shamed by my exposure.

These stanzas, addressed to his ideal of beauty, as the most brilliant feature of his plays, are doubtless intended to give the readers of this poem, when its true authorship shall be discovered, a history of his fears and anxieties at the most critical moment of his public career, when fortune was seemingly changing, and all before him was bright with hope and promise. His seven years of obscurity and want in the cloisters of Gray's Inn were, as he thought, to be changed for an active life in the courts of Westminster.

His ambition for office, wealth, and title could now, he felt, have a basis to work upon, which would insure its ultimate triumph. There was nothing in his way but the dreaded effects of a possible disclosure of his connection with the theatre, and his labors as a playwright. That would destroy his prospects, and consign his name to obloquy. In this day, with these dramas in the fore front of all the literature that has been produced in all the years since they were written, it seems incredible indeed that their presentation to the world should have been through falsehood, abandonment, and tribulation. The only man of that time who could appreciate the dramas, and forecast their destiny, was Bacon himself, and he was compelled by the force of circumstances to sacrifice them, or they would have sacrificed him. He knew they must immortalize some name; they could never live without a sponsor, and he conferred that honor, the noblest in the world of letters, upon Shakespeare, hoping and believing that in some of the ages before him it would return, and give him his true place among the greatest of the world's benefactors.

SONNET 73.

That time of year Thou mayst in Me behold
When yellow leaves, or none, or few, do hang
Upon those boughs which shake against the cold,
Bare ruin'd choirs, where late the sweet birds sang.

In Me Thou seest the twilight of such day
As after sunset fadeth in the west,
Which by and by black night doth take away,
Death's second self, that seals up all in rest.
In Me Thou seest the glowing of such fire
That on the ashes of his youth doth lie,
As the death-bed whereon it must expire,
Consum'd with that which it was nourish'd by.
This Thou perceiv'st, which makes Thy Love more strong,
To love that well which Thou must leave ere long.

This stanza, addressed to Thou (Truth), declares his unfitness for work in the condition he depicts for himself. He is like a late autumn,—a tree to whose boughs a few faded leaves are still clinging, abandoned by the birds that were wont to sing there. He is like a twilight from which the sunlight had faded, and darkness like death will soon overwhelm. "In me Thou seest the glowing of such fire that on the ashes of his youth doth lie" (his desire for writing is weakened, he cannot infuse the same energy and brightness into his productions that he did before his prospects for preferment came). "As the death-bed whereon it must expire" (he is losing all taste and inclination to write, and thinks he will never do it again). "Consumed with that which it was nourished by" (he was taught in youth to look to the offices and honors of public life as the reward of his studies and travels; and was educated with those objects in view. He was now, as he believed, about to realize these promises, and they absorbed his entire time, so that he had none to give to writing).

"This thou perceiv'st, which makes thy love more strong, to love that well which Thou must leave ere long" (his love of writing as an occupation had been a passion, and leaving it even for office would be a great sacrifice of happiness. This feeling grew upon him as the time for its indulgence lessened).

SONNET 74.

But be contented: when that fell arrest
Without all bail shall carry Me away,
My life hath in this line some interest,
Which for memorial still with Thee shall stay.
When Thou reviewest this, Thou dost review
The very part was consecrate to Thee:
The earth can have but earth, which is his due;
My spirit is Thine, the better part of Me.
So then thou hast but lost the dregs of life,
The prey of worms, My body being dead,
The coward conquest of a wretch's knife,
Too base of Thee to be remembered.
The worth of that is that which it contains,
And that is this, and this with Thee remains.

He promises in this stanza, when he is appointed solicitor-general, to leave this poem as a memorial of his dramas. "But be contented, when that fell arrest without all bail shall carry me away" (when he goes to fill the office, which requires his personal services, and cannot be supplied by another). "My life hath in this line some interest, which for memorial still with Thee shall stay" (the "interest" was the preservation in this poem of a history (memorial) of the part he had performed in the production of the dramas, which the world sooner or later would, by means of that history, discover and understand). "When Thou reviewest this, Thou dost review the very part was consecrate to Thee" (this poem, when understood, will be found to contain nothing but the truth). "The earth can have but earth, which is his due" (his body will die, dissolve, and be forgotten or uncared for). "My spirit is Thine, the better part of Me" (the soul and spirit which through that body created the dramas, the only part of him worth saving, is Thou's, Truth's). "So then thou hast but lost the dregs of life, the prey of worms, my body being dead" (in case of either going away, or actually dying, nothing of any value is lost by Thou as long as this poem is preserved). "The coward conquest of a wretch's knife, too base of Thee to be remembered" (this alludes to a period in Bacon's life when the indignation of the friends of Essex was roused against him for his speeches at the trial of that nobleman. His life had been threatened, and his friends thought he was in danger of secret assassination).

In a letter addressed to "Lord Henry Howard, clearing himself of aspersion in the case of the Earl of Essex," in 1599, Bacon says: "For my part, I have desired better than to have my name objected to envy, or my life to a ruffian's violence. But I have the privy coat of a good conscience."

A little later he writes to Sir Robert Cecil, concluding thus: "As to any violence to be offered to me, wherewith my friends tell me, with no small terror, I am threatened, I thank God I have the privy coat of a good conscience, and have long since put off any fearful care of life or the accidents of life." To the queen he writes, about the same time: "My life has been threatened and my name libelled, which I account an honour."

"The worth of that" (his body) "is that which it contains, and that is this" (the Sonnets), "and this with Thee" (his thoughts) "remains" (the worth of that "interest" above alluded to is the history contained in this poem, which, being the truth, will not be lost).

Sonnet 75.

So are You to My thoughts as food to life,
Or as sweet-season'd showers are to the ground;
And for the peace of You I hold such strife
As 'twixt a miser and his wealth is found:
Now proud as an enjoyer, and anon
Doubting the filching age will steal his treasure;
Now counting best to be with You alone,
Then better'd that the world may see My pleasure;
Sometime all full with feasting on Your sight,
And by and by clean starved for a look;
Possessing or pursuing no delight,
Save what is had or must from You be took.
  Thus do I pine and surfeit day by day,
  Or gluttoning on all, or all away.

He tells Beauty in this stanza of his delight when thinking of him, or seeing him in representation and in reading. As food is necessary to preserve life, and summer showers to refresh the earth, so is beauty needful to invigorate his mind. His love for him is like the love of a miser for his gold, — at one time proud of his delineation, then fearful that he may be robbed of his attractiveness by others. He is pleased to contemplate him in private; he affords food for conversation, and like a feast which fills him with delicacies, feasts his eyes and heart to the full in theatrical representations. "And by and by clean starved for a look" (when sometime absent from his thought he becomes eager for his recall). And "day by day" all his delight is in his presence, and all his misery in his absence.

SONNET 76.

Why is my verse so barren of new pride,
So far from variation or quick change?
Why, with the time, do I not glance aside
To new-found methods and to compounds strange?
Why write I still all one, ever the same,
And keep invention in a noted weed,
That every word doth almost tell My name,
Showing their birth, and where they did proceed?
O, know, sweet love, I always write of You,
And You and love are still My argument;
So all My best is dressing old words new,
Spending again what is already spent:
For as the sun is daily new and old,
So is My Love still telling what is told.

In this stanza he tells his name. "Why is my verse so barren of new pride, so far from variation and quick change?" (why in this poem does he not announce some new achievements of his pen, which like those of other writers for the stage sacrifice truth and beauty to the public taste for variety and sudden changes and effects in theatrical portraiture? Why not, in imitation of them, find something new and strange, and compound a play instead of adhering to the same straightforward course with which he commenced, of presenting the one great theme, Truth, in all that he writes?) "And keep invention in a noted weed, that every word doth almost tell my name" (Bacon found constant use in all his writings, as well those he acknowledged as the plays attributed to Shakespeare, for the word "invention." It contained wider meaning for him than any other word in the language, and the offices attributed to it in philosophy are fully analyzed and discussed in the "Advancement of Learning." Its greatest power was in origination, and understood in that sense, it was the power by which the plays were created). This he says he kept in a "noted weed." The only weed of which history gives account in Elizabeth's time was tobacco. It was introduced into England by some of the crews who returned from the first expedition to Virginia, fitted out by Sir Walter Raleigh. Its use by Raleigh soon popularized it among the nobility and upper classes. When James I. ascended the throne, smoking was so prevalent that in dread of its effects upon his subjects, the king himself denounced its use in a strong essay entitled "A Counterblast against Tobacco." Camden also published a powerful argument against its use.

Orthography in those days was unsettled. Words were spelled by sound rather than by rule, and generally the best scholars adopted rules of their own. The word "tobacco," by its various forms of pronunciation, was blessed with an orthography that would fill a small dictionary. The following furnish a few of the varieties: Tobaco, tobacco, tobaca, tobacy, tobaccy, 'bacco, 'bacy, etc., *ad infinitum.* The second syllable was as perfect then as now.

Bacon, by confession in this stanza, must have enjoyed his pipe. It soothed him, quieted his nerves, and favored that composure of the faculties needful to reflection and invention. It was undoubtedly his habit to resort to it in the hours given to the creation of his great dramas. It was in the placidity which it imparted to his system and the meditative mood it inspired that he virtually "kept invention." His thoughts were clearer, his plots better in development, and his poesy more exuberant than they would have been without this sedative.

In every form which spelling gave to tobacco, it *almost* told the name of Bacon. This evidence of the true origin of the dramas of Shakespeare, written by their author and published nearly three centuries ago, during Shakespeare's life, cannot by any force of logic or ingenuity be destroyed. It is unargumentable. It imparts the force of truth to this entire history, and relieves it of the suggestion, improbable in itself, that Shakespeare, for aught that appears, might have written it himself. No other name can fill the requirements of the line but that of Bacon. No anagram could be constructed which would avoid that conclusion connected with the lines preceding and following it. How plain, then, does it appear that Bacon alone was the author, when we connect the announcement made in this stanza with those parts of the poem which describe his compulsory attendance upon the queen, after his appointment as counsel extraordinary; his long months of suspense, sorrow, and disappointment spent in the effort to obtain the office of solicitor-general, and his transfer of the dramas to "Will" (Shakespeare),—matters which could not possibly have formed any part of Shakespeare's life.

Aside from other evidences the poem may contain, the appearance of Bacon's name shows a deliberate purpose in him to reveal himself to posterity as the author of the dramas. He would not otherwise have written this stanza, or for that matter this poem, for both were unnecessary for any other purpose. The poem, with the exception of a few stanzas, has no special merit, and being entirely unintelligible and silly without interpretation of some kind, no such person as the author of the great dramas would have written it for mere pastime. All former interpretations it has received have been nearly as incomprehensible as the bare poem itself. They tell no credible, no consecutive, story; make Shakespeare a licentious fool, and hold him up before the world as the vilest kind of a *debauchee*, and most unprincipled of men among men, on his own confession. This cannot be true. Regarding it as an allegory which contains the history of the great dramas, and those parts of it which cursorily considered convey a prurient meaning, as parts illustrative of the circumstances and conditions under which those dramas were written, it becomes a work of the greatest possible importance, full of interest and worth, and invaluable in the history it reveals of the greatest works in all literature.

Half the persons accused of and tried for the highest crimes known to our laws have been convicted and punished on much weaker testimony than is herein contained in proof of Bacon's authorship. Great lawyer as he was, Bacon was not unmindful of this, and shaped his narrative accordingly. The only fault that can be found with it is, that he succeeded too well in eluding detection, and reared an image which has been so long and so universally idolized, that it has become easier for the world to cling to the false worship than to receive the real divinity.

"O, know, sweet Love, I always write of You, and You and Love are still My argument" (he always wrote of Beauty, and at this time he was writing of beauty and love conjoined), from which I infer that the particular play upon which he was engaged was "Romeo and Juliet," which White seems to think was written in 1596. If I have conjectured rightly, it was written in 1594, just previous to the time he engaged in the strife for the solicitorship, which required all his energies. In view of any possible clew it might furnish to his exposure as a playwright, it may have been withheld from the stage until 1596, several months after his defeat. "So all my best is dressing old words new, spending again what is already spent" (this play is founded upon a novel written by Matteo Bandello, and published in 1554, so that it was indeed a "dressing old words new," etc.). "My love" (his dramas), like the sun, new in the morning, old in the evening, unites the old and the new in her composition. I think that "invention" in the sixth line was written by the author in the plural. It is the antecedent referred to in the eighth line, which being plural, should determine its number. A slight oversight of the proof-reader reasonably accounts for the mistake. "Showing their birth, and where they did proceed," can allude only to the "inventions" or dramas, as contrasted with the "new-found methods" and "compounds strange" of other writers of "the time." This view is strengthened by the two succeeding lines:—

> "O, know, sweet Love, I always write of You,
> And You and Love are *still* My argument."

He was "still" at the time delineating Love and Beauty in the same comedy.

Sonnet 77.

> Thy glass will show Thee how Thy beauties wear,
> Thy dial how Thy precious minutes waste;
> The vacant leaves Thy mind's imprint will bear,
> And of this book this learning mayst Thou taste.
> The wrinkles which Thy glass will truly show
> Of mouthed graves, will give Thee memory;
> Thou, by Thy dial's shady stealth mayst know
> Time's thievish progress to eternity.
> Look, what Thy memory cannot contain
> Commit to these waste blanks, and Thou shalt find
> Those children nurs'd, deliver'd from Thy brain,
> To take a new acquaintance of Thy mind.
> These offices, so oft as Thou wilt look,
> Shall profit Thee, and much enrich Thy book.

This stanza is descriptive of his initiatory labor in the preparation for writing a drama.

"Thy glass" alludes to and signifies public opinion. This will determine whether the truth and beauty supplied by Thy (Thought), when transformed by Thou (Truth) into the dramas, will be of permanent or temporary interest. "Thy dial," the indicator of time's flight, will show him the value of moments in this work. "The vacant leaves" (the blank paper upon which his thoughts are to be written for preservation and reference). "This book," composed of fugutive thoughts and collected learning, is to be tested as it progresses by Thou (Truth). "The wrinkles of mouthed graves," which his glass will truly show, are such selections as he may choose from the writings of the learned men and sages of former ages, being still reminded by the dial of the flight of time. Those that he cannot remember he must transcribe in his book. He will find that they will aid greatly in giving substance and force to his own thoughts when he arranges them in form for use. The true value of "these offices" will be demonstrated when, under the guidance of Thou (Truth), they are applied to the faithful delineation of life and character. It will be seen from this stanza what his leading methods were in the composition of the dramas: first, he gave his own thoughts to the work, careful to make his plots as natural as possible. Then he used the thoughts of others to strengthen his own, and not transcend the truth. It required the mind and skill of a master to succeed in this species of composition, and any one who would adopt it should be conscious of possessing the imagery, brain, cultivation, and application of Bacon before he begins, or he will be sure to end in ridiculous failure. He says as much himself in the two following stanzas.

Sonnet 78.

So oft have I invok'd Thee for My Muse,
And found such fair assistance in My verse,
As every alien pen hath got My use,
And under Thee their poesy disperse.
Thine eyes, that taught the dumb on high to sing
And *heavy ignorance* aloft to fly,
Have added feathers to the learned's wing,
And given grace *a double majesty.*
Yet be most proud of that which I compile,
Whose influence is Thine and born of Thee:
In others' works Thou dost but mend the style,
And arts with thy sweet graces, graced be;
But Thou art all My art, and dost advance
As high as learning My *rude ignorance.*

In this stanza he alludes to a play which was the production of several writers of the period, himself included. "Every alien pen," he says, has got his use. They are all striving to imitate him. "And under Thee [Thought] their poesy disperse." It is noticeable that he gives them no credit for Thou (Truth).

As a contrast to their efforts, he tells what Thou (Truth) has done. "Thine [Truth] eyes, that taught the dumb on high [himself (Bacon) of noble parentage, and a nobleman in expectancy] to sing."s By birth and position he was entitled to move in the highest circles, socially and in public life. "And heavy ignorance [Shakespeare, a man without education or culture] aloft to fly" (to enjoy the renown and adulation which, as the imputed author of the dramas, followed him). "Thine eyes" (this Truth), that has done so much for him and Shakespeare, has also "added feathers to the learned's wing" (it has contributed to the literary labors of writers of learning and education), "and given grace a double majesty." This allusion to "double majesty" must have been the second and third parts of King Henry VI. Guizot is of opinion that Shakespeare was "almost entirely a stranger" to the first part of Henry VI. He says: "'The True History of the Contention' and 'The True Tragedy of Richard, Duke of York,'—one served as a matrix, if I may be allowed the expression, for the second part of Henry VI., and the other for the third part." The "True History" and "The True Tragedy" were performed as early as 1592. Robert Green, one of the authors, died in September of that year. They were rewritten afterwards, with many changes and additions, and appeared as the second and third parts of Henry VI.

The graceful style of the original plays, supposed to be the conjoint productions of Peele, Green, Marlow, and Shakespeare (or, as I say, Bacon), was what Bacon alluded to by the word "grace" in the line under consideration. "Thine eyes" (Truth) gave to this "grace" "a double majesty,"—that is, changed it to the two parts of Henry VI.

The contention among the numerous commentators upon Shakespeare, from Theobald down to the present day, concerning the authorship of these plays, has been quite as persistent, and in some instances nearly as bitter, as the contention illustrated by the plays themselves. The preponderance of the multitudinous opinions favors a joint authorship for the plays originally by Shakespeare, Marlow, Peele, and Green, the last three learned men and collegians. In an able essay, White very clearly recognizes the style of each. This was probably the work alluded to in the eighty-sixth stanza, which, as the "affable, familiar ghost," Shakespeare assisted by contributing such passages as Bacon supplied.

Bacon represents the "alien pen" as using Thee (Thought) only, and himself as illustrating Thou (Truth). He asks Thought "to be most proud of that part of the play which he compiles, because, though born of thought, it is written under the influence of truth. In that part written by the others, truth has only mended their style, and thought given grace to their art; but truth has been all his art, and has enabled him "to advance as high as learning My rude ignorance" (to place Shakespeare on an equality with them as a writer).

Sonnet 79.

Whilst I alone did call upon Thy aid,
My verse alone had all Thy gentle grace,
But now My gracious numbers are decay'd,
And My sick Muse doth give another place.
I grant, sweet love, Thy lovely argument
Deserves the travail of a worthier pen,

Yet what of Thee Thy poet doth invent
He robs Thee of and pays it Thee again.
He lends Thee virtue, and he stole that word
From Thy behaviour; beauty doth he give,
And found it in Thy cheek; he can afford
No praise to Thee but what in Thee doth live.
  Then thank him not for that which he doth say,
  Since what he owes Thee Thou Thyself dost pay.

In this stanza he conveys the idea that, having ceased to write, another writer has taken his place, and it would seem is also writing under the sanction of Shakespeare's name. When he was the only writer who used Thy (Thought), "My verse," (this poem spoke of his own works only). "But now My gracious numbers are decay'd" (now that he has ceased to write dramas), "My sick Muse" (he reluctantly) "doth give another place" (announces a successor): "I grant, sweet love, Thy lovely argument" (the preparation which his successor has made for his play) "deserves the travail of a worthier pen" (deserves a better delineation than he has given it). Yet so much of it as he has taken from Thought, he has returned to Thought again. The virtue which he has represented he took from Thy (Thought), and the beauty that he gives to his characters he found in him. His drama is entitled to no praise for any merit, that he did not find in the material which he collected from others for its construction. In other words, it has no originality, and all that "he owes Thee" (the preparation) "Thou [Truth],

Thyself doth pay." Thought has been put in form, but without any power of beauty or truth on the part of the writer, and is of no more value than it was before it was transposed from the crude material. This is as much as to say, that if he had used the same material he would have produced a much better play.

SONNET 80.

O, how I faint when I of You do write,
Knowing a better spirit doth use Your name,
And in the praise thereof spends all his might,
To make Me tongue-tied, speaking of Your fame!
But since Your worth, wide as the ocean is,
The humble as the proudest sail doth bear,
My saucy bark, inferior far to his,
On your broad main doth wilfully appear.
Your shallowest help will hold Me up afloat,
Whilst he upon Your soundless deep doth ride;
Or, being wrack'd, I am a worthless boat,
He of *tall building and of goodly pride.*
  Then if he thrive and I be cast away,
  The worst was this, — My Love was My decay.

In this stanza he informs us that he (Bacon) is studiously pursuing his philosophical inquiries. "O, how I [Bacon as dramatist] faint when I of You do write, knowing a better spirit [Bacon as philosopher] doth use Your name" (the contrast here suggested is between Beauty (You) in poetry and Beauty in philosophy, the one, everything externally attractive, and the other full of power internally, and much superior in strength and self-assertion). "And in the praise thereof spends all his might" (all his power of research, logic, invention, and illustration are employed to demonstrate truth and beauty in philosophy). "To make Me [dramatist] tongue-tied, speaking of Your fame" (those labors will show wherein the plays are deficient in demonstrating and enforcing truth into the practice of mankind). But since "Your worth" (your truth) is an ocean upon which vessels of every size and cost may sail, "My saucy bark" (his poetry and plays) will not be deprived of this right. "Your shallowest help will hold Me [dramatist] up afloat" (his dramas need no deep philosophical investigation of beauty for their ornamentation). "Whilst he [philosopher] upon Your soundless deep doth ride" (his philosophy, on the contrary, will be of the most profound nature). If his dramas should fail, it would be comparatively unimportant, as his philosophy is more exhaustive, built up higher in argument, and will go before the world in "goodly pride" (with the name of Francis Bacon as author, which from his position will give it character). "The worst" of it is, that if the philosophy succeeds and the dramas fail, it will be because "My Love was My decay" (because he had over-estimated his powers of delineation).

SONNET 81.

Or shall I live Your epitaph to make,
Or You survive when I in earth am rotten;
From hence Your memory death cannot take,
Although in Me each part will be forgotten.

Your name from hence immortal life shall have,
Though I, once gone, to all the world must die;
The earth can yield Me but a common grave,
When You entomb'd in men's eyes shall lie.
Your monument shall be My gentle verse,
Which eyes not yet created shall o'er-read,
And tongues to be Your being shall rehearse
When all the breathers of this world are dead;
  You still shall live — such virtue hath my pen —
  Where breath most breathes, even in the mouths of men.

In this stanza he assures himself that if his dramas outlive him they will live forever. "Or shall I live Your epitaph to make." This seems to be a closing up of the latter part of the line in the preceding stanza, and means simply as opposed to that (or he will outlive his dramas). "Or You survive when I in earth am rotten" (or though he should die, their beauty will preserve them, so that they will live when he is forgotten). Beauty will be immortal in them, though he be dead "to all the world." His remains will fill a common grave, but the beauty of his dramas will be seen by all people. This poem shall give their history, and shall be read by the men of future ages, and they shall write and talk about your beauty when the present generation has ceased to exist. He had written so truly, and illustrated life so perfectly, that he should be best known and appreciated where the greatest numbers dwell. This is but one of several prophecies in this poem foretelling its unending life, which has been in the course of a continuous fulfilment ever since it was written.

SONNET 82.

I grant Thou wert not married to My Muse,
And therefore mayst without attaint o'erlook
The dedicated words which writers use
Of their fair subject, blessing every book.
Thou art as fair in knowledge as in hue,
Finding Thy worth a limit past My praise,
And therefore art enforc'd to seek anew
Some fresher stamp of the time-bettering days.
And do so, love; yet when they have devis'd
What strained touches rhetoric can lend,
Thou truly fair wert truly sympathiz'd
In true plain words by Thy *true-telling* friend;
And their gross painting might be better us'd
Where cheeks need blood; in Thee it is abus'd.

In this stanza, in the form of an apology to Thou (Truth) for neglecting to write a dedication in the style and fashion of the times, he furnishes a key which unfolds the true meaning of the dedicatory words prefixed to this poem. Thou (Truth), being as accessible to all as to him, could very properly overlook the want of a dedication. The worth of his thoughts surpassed any effort he might make to praise Thy, and he must look for his eulogy in the works of more recent writers. But he would find after the search, notwithstanding their strained efforts, that Thou's (Truth's) merits had been fully appreciated and set forth "in true plain words by Thy [Thought's] *true-telling* friend." The "gross painting" of other writers could be much better applied to subjects that stood in need of praise. It was only belittling Thee (Thought) to squander it on him.

Those "true plain words" have puzzled the heads of more writers during the past three centuries than any equal number of "true plain words" in the English language. It cannot be deemed presumptuous in me to attempt an interpretation which has foiled so many, for if I fail too, I shall die in the best of company. The lines just quoted tell that the poems are dedicated to Thou, or that Thou is the one "sympathiz'd" by the dedication. That furnishes the key to its exposition. Mr. W. H., the person seemingly addressed, fills a subordinate place. This is the language as it was written originally:—

TO · THE · ONLIE · BEGETTER · OF ·
THESE · INSVING · SONNETS ·
Mr. W. H. ALL · HAPPINESSE ·
AND · THAT · ETERNITIE ·
PROMISED ·
BY ·
OVR · EVER-LIVING · POET ·
WISHETH ·
THE · WELL-WISHING ·
ADVENTVRER · IN ·
SETTING ·
FORTH ·
T. T.

I read the dedication thus:—

"MR. W. H. WISHETH THAT ETERNITY PROMISED BY OUR EVER-LIVING POET, TO THE ONLY BEGETTER OF THESE ENSUING SONNETS, AND ALL HAPPINESS TO THE WELL-WISHING ADVENTURER IN SETTING FORTH T. T. (THE TRUTH)."

Thou (Truth) is claimed and represented by the poet from the commencement to the close of the poem to be its "only begetter." Thy is the thought that puts the truth in form. Beauty is used as an ornament only. The poem narrates the truth concerning the dramas, their origin, and the reasons for their appearance as the works of Shakespeare. What matters it who "Mr. W. H." or who "the well-wishing adventurer" is? They are evidently used or assumed to conceal the real purpose of the dedication; probably, like the rest of it, entirely allegorical. That T. T. means The Truth, instead of Thomas Thorpe, as generally believed, is seemingly, at least, refigured in the alliteration, "*true telling*," in the foregoing lines, and without some close akin to it, it is impossible to complete the sense of the dedication.

What is the evidence that Thomas Thorpe ever existed? The following entry in the Stationer's Register, under the date of May 20, 1609, is all:—

> "THOMAS THORPE.—Entred for his copie under th[e h]andes of master Wilson and master Lownes Warden, a Booke called Shakespeare's *sonnettes*, vjd."

By this it appears that the entry for his copyright was made and paid for "by the hands of Master Wilson and Master Lownes, Warden." History is silent as to who they were, or at whose request they made the entry. No writer has been able to solve the mystery attending the publication of the Sonnets. The prevailing opinion is, that they were surreptitiously obtained and published without authority. This is hardly probable. If these interpretations are correct, Bacon contrived the plan for their publication, and found in Thomas Thorpe a man of his own creation, the two initials (T. T.) signifying The Truth placed at the close of his enigmatical dedication.

SONNET 83.

I never saw that You did painting need,
And therefore to Your fair no painting set;
I found, or thought I found, You did exceed
The barren tender of a poet's debt;
And therefore have I slept in Your report,
That You Yourself, being extant, well might show
How far a modern quill doth come too short,
Speaking of worth, what worth in You doth grow.
This silence, for My sin You did impute,
Which shall be most my glory, being dumb;
For I impair not beauty, being mute,
When others would give life and bring a tomb.
  There lives more life in one of Your fair eyes
  Than both Your poets can in praise devise.

In this stanza he gives his reasons for not including Beauty in the dedication. He saw no reason for praising him, because all effort to do so would be so greatly excelled by Beauty himself, that the praise would be "barren" and meaningless. He had not done it, because Beauty of himself and in delineation would demonstrate by his presence how impossible it would be for any writer to do justice to his merits, and speak of him as he is, or as he will be appreciated by his constant growth. It has been imputed to him by Beauty, in the writings of others, that it was wrong to publish his poem without an intelligible dedication, but he was glad he had not written one, as by being silent he had not impaired Beauty, while others, who expected great benefit from their dedications, had effectually ruined their works by them. There was more "life" (more to give Beauty perpetuity) in one of Your delineations than any praise that both he and his successor could possibly "devise."

SONNET 84.

Who is it that says most? which can say more
Than this rich praise, that You alone are You?
In whose confine immured is the store
Which should example where Your equal grew.
Lean penury within that pen doth dwell
That to his subject lends not some small glory;
But he that writes of You, if he can tell
That You are You, so dignifies his story.
Let him but copy what in You is writ,
Not making worse what nature made so clear,
And such a counterpart shall fame his wit,
Making his style admired everywhere.
You to Your beauteous blessings add a curse,
Being fond on praise, which makes Your praises worse.

In this stanza he enlarges upon the merits of Beauty when considered by himself. How is it possible to exceed the praise of a thing which is commended to all your faculties by its beauty. To feel that it is beautiful, and call it so, is the utmost limit of praise. It contains in itself an example for all. He is a poor writer, who, however he borrows from others, imparts no interest from his own thoughts to his subject. But if he writes to illustrate anything beautiful, and it is recognized in that sense, his story needs no other praise. Let him follow nature in his delineation, and his work will be "admired everywhere." Beauty which seeks praise outside of itself, deprives its own intrinsic merit of full appreciation.

SONNET 85.

My tongue-tied Muse in manners holds her still,
While comments of your praise, richly compil'd,
Reserve their character with golden quill
And precious phrase by all the Muses fil'd.
I think good thoughts, whilst others write good words,
And, like unletter'd clerk, still cry "Amen"
To every hymn that able spirit affords
In polish'd form of well-refined pen.
Hearing You prais'd, I say, "'T is so, 't is true,
And to the most of praise add something more;
But that is in My thought, whose love to You,
Though words come hindmost, holds his rank before.
Then others for the breath of words respect,
Me for My dumb thoughts, speaking in effect.

In this stanza he agrees in thought with those who add praise to beauty in their poems, but writes nothing in his praise himself. His muse is quiet in that respect, because it would be in direct violation of his views already expressed, to write in praise of a subject which needed no praise; in other words, it would be superfluous "to gild refined gold and paint the lily." All the other poets are devoting their best efforts to this purpose. He thinks as highly of beauty as they who write in his praise, he assents to all that his accomplished successor may say of Beauty by a casual remark of approval. To this, however, in his thought he adds a higher adoration, which is embodied in thought rather than words. If those who write are to be respected for their eulogies of beauty, he claims equal honor for the creation he has given her in thoughts, which is more effective.

SONNET 86.

Was it the proud full sail of his great verse,
Bound for the prize of all too precious You,
That did My ripe thoughts in My brain inhearse,
Making their tomb the womb wherein they grew?
Was it his spirit, by spirits taught to write
Above a mortal pitch, that struck Me dead?
No, neither He, nor His compeers by night,
Giving Him aid, My verse astonished.
He, nor that affable familiar ghost
Which nightly gulls Him with intelligence,
As victors of My silence cannot boast;
I was not sick of any fear from thence:
But when Your countenance fill'd up his line,
Then lack'd I matter; that enfeebled Mine.

In this stanza he tells the reason why he has ceased to continue writing for the present. Was it the ambitious character of the poetry of his successor, or the pursuit and capture of Beauty, which was its object, that caused him to suppress the utterance of thoughts he had already formed? Was it the spiritual nature of his poesy, which "above a mortal pitch" exceeded all ordinary powers of comprehension that silenced him? No, neither that, nor the assistance which he nightly received from others, depreciated his own verses. Nor did the amiable, good-natured interloper who cheated them with "intelligence" have any influence in silencing him. What, then, was it? It was that by giving him surreptitious assistance he saw his own poetry in another's work. That deprived him of material for his labors, and rendered him powerless to pursue them. It was the "countenance" (the real beauty of his own thoughts), not the beauty of words, which made him suspend work.

This poet, who for some unexplained reason he treats as his successor, may have been Daniel, Marlow, Peele, or Chapman. Next to Shakespeare, they were regarded as the best poets and playwrights of the period. Instigated by the cordial welcome with which the dramas purporting to be Shakespeare's were received by the public, they, as is intimated in a former stanza, attempted to imitate them. It is probably not saying too much for Bacon, to attribute to the influence of his dramas the great change which at this time occurred in dramatic composition. New subjects were chosen, and an entirely new face put upon the forms of representation. If Bacon had not written, the dramas of Marlow and Peele would have immortalized the age, so great and admirable were their powers of poetic delineation.

I think that one of the four above named was at the time referred to in the stanza engaged in writing a play in which he was assisted by the others, or some of them. Shakespeare, whom Robert Green the playwright called a Johannes Factotum, knew and informed Bacon of it. Ascertaining the subject and drift of the play through Shakespeare, Bacon may have from time to time, while the work was progressing, plied Shakespeare with facts and occasional descriptions which Shakespeare, as the "affable familiar ghost," and recognized by the others as the popular playwright of the time, communicated to them, and they incorporated them into the play. He thus "gull'd" them with the matter supplied by Bacon. And afterwards when the play appeared, and Bacon saw and heard his own lines repeated in it, he became disgusted, and concluded that he would cease writing at once, as he must do so very soon, at any rate, if he succeeded in obtaining the position of solicitor. This can hardly be called a forced conclusion, when we remember that for purposes of concealment, it was as necessary that Shakespeare should be favorably known and appreciated among his associates as that Bacon should be by his friends. Shakespeare had been accused of plagiarism as early as 1592 by Green, in his "Groatesworth of Wit," who in an address to Marlow, Lodge, and Peele, written on his death-bed, says, in allusion to Shakespeare:—

"There is an upstart crow beautiful with our feathers, that with his tiger's heart, wrapt in a player's hide, supposes he is as well able to bombast out a blank verse as the best of you, and being an absolute Johannes Factotum, is in his own conceit the only Shake-scene in the country. O, that I might entreat your rare wits to be employed in more profitable courses; and let those apes imitate your past excellence, and never more acquaint them with your admired inventions."

Bacon well knew that Shakespeare's authorship among these accomplished writers required constant watchfulness on his part to avoid exposure, as that would betray him. This fear, constantly before him, must have led to many strange devices, the one above conjectured probably, among the rest.

The motive which he gives of "lacking matter" would have little weight with one so fruitful in resources, but seeing the "countenance" (his own thoughts) intermixed with those of his successor, as he dubs him, he might well take alarm, lest others, observing the difference in the style of the play, should stir up inquiry, which would cause him to be suspected. When he was assigned by Queen Elizabeth as one of the counsel to conduct the inquiry concerning the conduct of the Earl of Essex in Ireland, and told, as he writes in an explanatory letter afterwards, "that I should set forth some undutiful carriage of my lord in giving occasion and countenance to a seditious pamphlet, as it was termed, which was dedicated unto him, which was the book before mentioned of King Henry IV. Whereupon I replied to that allotment, and said to their lordships that it was an old matter, and had no manner of coherence with the rest of the charge, being matters of Ireland; and therefore that I, having been wronged by bruits before, this would expose me to them more, and it would be said that I gave in evidence *mine own tales.*" From this passage it is apparent that he had been suspected of writing the play of Henry IV. How else than from Shakespeare would he have been likely to know of the nightly meetings of these poets, and the work they were doing? He had no personal intercourse with them, was not in their secrets, and all his writings for the theatre were veiled by Shakespeare. Yet he is able in this history to give the whole story, and to mention as an "affable familiar ghost," one who "gulls them with intelligence" (who gives them as of himself what he has received from another). Does not this mean Shakespeare?

Sonnet 87.

Farewell! Thou art too dear for my possessing,
And like enough Thou know'st Thy estimate:
The charter of Thy worth gives Thee releasing;
My bonds in Thee are all determinate.
For how do I hold Thee but by Thy granting?
And for that riches where is My deserving?
The cause of this fair gift in Me is wanting,
And so My patent back again is swerving.
Thyself Thou gav'st, Thy own worth then not knowing,
Or Me, to whom Thou gav'st it, else mistaking;
So Thy great gift, upon *misprision* growing,
Comes home again, on better judgment making.
  Thus have I had Thee, as a dream doth flatter,
  In sleep a king, but waking no such matter.

The farewell in this stanza means that his dramatic labors must cease. Thou (Truth) is now so much sought after by the playwrights that his exclusive use of him is gone. In the use which others make of him, it is very probable that the labors of Thy (Thought) will be found wanting. But Thy must be released also, for he has no longer use for him, and he can only hold him while he is willing. So long as he will not write dramas, Thy is unnecessary,—the cause or object of his creation no longer remains with him,—and so the "patent" which he devised for weaving Thy into his labors has ceased to interest him. Thou (Truth) was the substance of Thy (Thought). Thought, when awakened in him, did not know his power, but this knowledge came to him afterwards, and with the help of Thou he grew by "misprision" (concealed truths and phrases). Now, with the approval of his own judgment, Thy returns to his inert condition. While he remained with him he made him proud and vain, ruled him as a king when he had no other work, but now a greater pursuit was before him, and Thy was bereft of his attractions.

The "patent," or plan of composition adopted by Bacon, has been already explained. The dissolution given to it in this stanza, and the motive assigned for it, show that Bacon had the fullest confidence in his appointment as solicitor, and would never occupy his time again in writing dramas. The prize he had toiled for was almost within his grasp, and his gloomy period of seclusion nearly over. The difficulties and obstructions he was confident would be overcome by his noble young friend, the Earl of Essex, who was giving all his energy, popularity, and powers of persuasion to his application. The story of those labors—of the opposing forces; of the delays; of the vacillating conduct of Elizabeth; of the duplicity of the Cecils; of the faithful devotion of Essex; and the final defeat of Bacon, in all running through seventeen months of the years 1594 and 1595—is much too long to be detailed here. There will be frequent occasion to refer to the effect it produced in Bacon's mind, while it was passing, in the consideration given to future Sonnets.

SONNET 88.

When Thou shalt be dispos'd to set Me light,
And place My merit in the eye of scorn,
Upon Thy side against Myself I 'll fight,
And prove Thee virtuous, though Thou art foresworn.
With Mine own weakness, being best acquainted,
Upon Thy part I can set down a story
Of faults conceal'd, wherein I am attainted,
That Thou in losing Me shalt win much glory:
And I by this will be a gainer too;
For bending all My loving thoughts on Thee,
The injuries that to Myself I do,
Doing Thee vantage, double-vantage Me.
Such is My love, to Thee I so belong,
That for Thy right Myself will bear all wrong.

If it should so happen that while seeking the appointment of solicitor-general, any charges should be arrayed against him by his enemies of a personal character, for the purpose of depreciating his merits and defeating him, he (Bacon as an individual) will defend the purity and virtue of Thy,—the thoughts embodied in the dramas,—by fighting against Myself (Bacon as author). His object will be to mislead his opponents and prevent them from suspecting that he had been a writer for the theatre. That fact, if proved against him, would not only defeat him, but drive him into hopeless obscurity. How would he prove Thy's purity? Knowing his own weakness, how the dramas were composed, and what means he had employed, he could "set down a story of faults conceal'd" of which he was guilty. He would show that the dramas were a compilation of truths, derived from infinite sources. All the great writers of all former ages had contributed to them. They had grown, as he says in the preceding stanza, by misprision, "faults concealed." Thou (Truth) would win much glory by such a revelation, because it would show that Bacon alone could not have been the author, but that the truth displayed was the product of ages. By thus exposing his patent, "bending all My loving thoughts on Thee," which of course would be done judiciously, he would divert attention from himself, and be a gainer also. Every injury he did to "Myself" (Bacon as author) would benefit Thee (Thought), and prove of double benefit to Bacon as a candidate. Such is My Love (the dramas), so are they composed, and he at this time is so absorbed in electioneering schemes that to obtain the office "Myself" (Bacon as the author) "will bear all wrong." In other words, he will by all possible means avoid exposure as the author of the dramas.

SONNET 89.

Say that Thou didst forsake Me for some fault,
And I will comment upon that offence;
Speak of My lameness, and I straight will halt,
Against Thy reasons making no defence.
Thou canst not, love, disgrace Me half so ill,
To set a form upon desired change,
As I'll Myself disgrace: knowing Thy will,
I will acquaintance strangle and look strange,

Be absent from Thy walks, and in My tongue
Thy sweet beloved name no more shall dwell,
Lest I (too much profane) should do it wrong,
And haply of our old acquaintance tell.
  For Thee against Myself I 'll vow debate,
  For I must ne'er love him whom Thou dost hate.

Continuing his address to Thou (Truth) in this stanza, he expresses the intention, even though errors may appear in the dramas, of abandoning them altogether to such fate as may be accorded them by the world. "Say that Thou didst forsake Me for some fault" (some passage or passages did not contain the truth), "and I will comment upon that offence" (he will consider the subject). "Speak of My lameness, and I straight will halt, against Thy reasons making no defence" (if the fault is in the metre, he will have no argument with Thou about it). "Thou canst not, love, disgrace Me half so ill, to set a form upon desired change, as I'll Myself disgrace" (any discovery of error which may require that a new form should be set up, or new edition printed to correct or change it, he will not regard). "Knowing Thy will" (knowing his own will to avoid exposure), "I will acquaintance strangle and look strange, be absent from Thy walks, and in My tongue Thy sweet beloved name no more shall dwell" (he will think no more on the subject, it shall be forgotten; he will never recall it, nor even mention it), "lest I (too much profane) should do it wrong, and haply of our old acquaintance tell" (lest he should be tempted to denounce it, or worse even, accidentally reveal himself as the author. For these reasons he would offer no defence for himself, or for his erroneous composition).

SONNET 90.

Then hate Me when Thou wilt,—if ever, now;
Now, while the world is bent My deeds to cross,
Join with the spite of fortune, make Me bow,
And do not drop in for an after-loss.
Ah, do not, when My heart hath scap'd this sorrow,
Come in the rearward of a conquer'd woe;
Give not a windy night a rainy morrow,
To linger out a purpos'd overthrow.
If Thou wilt leave Me, do not leave Me last,
When other petty griefs have done their spite,
But in the onset come; so shall I taste
At first the very worst of fortune's might,
And other strains of woe, which now seem woe,
Compar'd with loss of Thee will not seem so.

Pursuing the thread of allegory in this stanza, as if conscious of deserving the hatred of Truth for the resolution he has formed to neglect and abandon it, he invites Thou to his revenge. "Then hate Me when Thou wilt,—if ever, now; now, while the world is bent My deeds to cross." At this time Bacon was invoking aid from every quarter in support of his pretensions to the office of solicitor-general. His life had been so correct, so studious, so isolated, that nothing stronger could be urged against him than that he was not fitted by habits or pursuits for the position, and was extravagant in his expenses. These objections in themselves would probably, have been insufficient in the eyes of the queen, were there not others whispered in her ears by some secret enemy, tending to shake her faith in his competency. It was during this struggle that, in reply to one of the urgent solicitations of Essex in behalf of the appointment, she said: "Bacon had great wit and much learning, but that in the law he could show to the uttermost of his knowledge, and was not deep." Montagu says: "Essex was convinced that Bacon's enemy was the Lord-Keeper Puckering." Macaulay thinks "that Bacon himself attributed his defeat to his relations, Lord Burleigh and his son Sir Robert Cecil." He quotes the following remarkable passage from a letter written by Bacon to Villiers many years afterwards: "Countenance, encourage, and advance able men in all kinds, degrees, and professions. For in the time of the Cecils, the father and son, able men were of design and of purpose suppressed." While engaged in the effort to resist the effect of these and similar influences upon the mind of the queen, his fear of betrayal as a writer of plays must have haunted him like a spectre, to have revived so many years afterwards, such a vivid memory of it as he gives in this poem. In this spirit he invokes the hatred of Thou at that time, which is equivalent to saying that he wished all possible evidence of his dramas might be removed entirely from public observation.

They were created of Thou (Truth), and his hatred would conceal, while his love would expose him. "Join with the spite of fortune, make me bow" (as fortune was hostile to him, so mayst Thou be, that he may not hold him in fear; he will thank him for the favor). "Ah, do not, when my heart hath scap'd this sorrow, come in the rearward of a conquered woe" (do not reveal yourself after he has overcome other obstacles). "Give not a windy night a rainy morrow, to linger out a purpos'd overthrow" (do not follow up the darkness and noise which now envelops him with thy storm and clouds, to aid those who are working for his defeat). "If Thou wilt leave Me, do not leave Me last, when other petty griefs have done their spite" (let not this exposure of his authorship be made when other and weaker impediments are removed). "But in the onset come" (come as an enemy at first, and you will not be found out). "So shall I taste at first the very worst of fortune's might" (then with nothing to fear from you, all my fear will be of the calumnies of the day). "And other strains of woe, which now seem woe, compar'd with loss of Thee will not seem so" (they will not alarm him; the only fear he has is this exposure as a playwright, all other opposition is nothing in comparison). He was certain that he would be appointed if his labors for the stage could be kept in concealment.

SONNET 91.

Some glory in their birth, some in their skill,
Some in their wealth, some in their body's force,
Some in their garments, though new-fangled ill,
Some in their hawks and hounds, some in their horse;
And every humour hath his adjunct pleasure,
Wherein it finds a joy above the rest:
But these particulars are not My measure;
All these I better in one general best.
Thy love is better than high birth to Me,
Richer than wealth, prouder than garments' cost,
Of more delight than hawks or horses be;
And having Thee, of all men's pride I boast:
  Wretched in this alone, that Thou mayst take
  All this away and Me most wretched make.

He names in this stanza, as the highest enjoyment and greatest pride of his life, the time that he has spent in the creation of his dramas. There is for every one some particular pleasure paramount to all others; as for some their birth, others their skill. Some worship wealth, some strength. Fine garments, hawks, hounds, and horses have each their special admirers, who take their greatest pleasure in them. He has no choice among these, they are alike agreeable; but that which he prizes above them all is "Thy love" (the delight he has experienced in weaving his own true thought, and the truths gathered from the past, into the immortal dramas). In them, and in the truths of which they are composed, he has the pride of all men. It is depicted in them, and it saddens him when he thinks that in the attempts of others to illustrate truth, all its beauty may be destroyed.

SONNET 92.

But do Thy worst to steal Thyself away,
For term of life Thou art assured Mine,
And life no longer than Thy love will stay,
For it depends upon that love of Thine.
Then need I not to fear the worst of wrongs,
When in the least of them My life hath end.
I see a better state to Me belongs
Than that which on Thy humour doth depend;
Thou canst not vex Me with inconstant mind,
Since that My life on Thy revolt doth lie.
O, what a happy title do I find,
Happy to have Thy love, happy to die!
But what 's so blessed-fair that fears no blot?
Thou mayst be false, and yet I know it not.

In this stanza he expresses the conviction that Thou (Truth) will be with him during life. "But do Thy worst to steal Thyself away" (his delineated thoughts), "for term of life Thou art assured Mine" (Thou (Truth) will be with him while he lives), "and life no longer than Thy love will stay, for it depends upon that love of Thine" (all knowledge of him and his dramatic labors (his life) ceases (dies) when he stops writing (Thou's love of Thy ends); as from that moment they will be recognized as the work of Shakespeare). "Then need I not to fear the worst of wrongs" (which he declares to be the disappearance of Thy), "when in the least of them My life hath end" (since his name is gone from the moment he ceases to write). "I see a better state to me belongs" (he is sure of the appointment as solicitor), "than that which on Thy humour doth depend" (superior in rank and position to writing). "Thou canst not vex Me with inconstant mind, since that My life on Thy revolt doth lie" (he cannot be blamed for preferring this office to writing, as the disclosure of that would ruin him). He will gain a title (be ennobled) by it, retain possession of Thou (Truth), and be happy in a cessation of labor as a writer. Better than all Thy (his thoughts) being gone, there may be some untruths in his writings which cannot be discovered.

SONNET 93.

So shall I live, supposing Thou art true,
Like a deceived husband; so love's face
May still seem love to Me, though alter'd new,
Thy looks with Me, Thy heart in other place;
For there can live no hatred in Thine eye,
Therefore in that I cannot know Thy change.
In many's looks the false heart's history
Is writ in moods and frowns and wrinkles strange.
But heaven in Thy creation did decree
That in Thy face sweet love should ever dwell;
Whate'er Thy thoughts or Thy heart's workings be,
Thy looks should nothing thence but sweetness tell.
  How like Eve's apple doth Thy beauty grow,
  If Thy sweet virtue answer not Thy show!

He tells in this stanza that Truth will have the same attraction for him when his pursuit has changed as it had before. Ignorant of any falsity in Thou (Truth), as he says in the previous stanza, he will live supposing him to be true. His new position will seemingly, at least, have the same attraction for him, as, like a husband who knowing no wrong in his wife confides in her honesty, so he, seeing nothing in the office to prevent, will accept it, and find in the discharge of its duties much pleasure. In appearance Truth will be the same, though he may not display it in the same form. It is always the same, without change. There are many writers who in attempting its delination have strangely misconceived it. It was born of heaven pure and beautiful, and its appearance, whatever form it may assume, is full of beauty. If its influence is not equal to its appearance, it, like "Eve's apple," tempts but to destroy.

Sonnet 94.

They that have power to hurt and will do none,
That do not do the thing they most do show,
Who, moving others, are themselves as stone,
Unmoved, cold, and to temptation slow,
They rightly do inherit heaven's graces,
And husband nature's riches from expense;
They are the lords and owners of their faces,
Others but stewards of their excellence.
The summer's flower is to the summer sweet,
Though to itself it only live and die,
But if that flower with base infection meet,
The basest weed outbraves its dignity:
  For sweetest things turn sourest by their deeds:
  Lilies that fester smell far worse than weeds.

He describes a class of contemporary authors, whose writings are cold, impassive, and destitute of merit or influence. They possess ability, but do not display it; make great pretensions, but do not establish them; impart life to their personations, but are unfeeling themselves. Their finical sense of propriety overcomes their vigor of expression, and shields them from all temptation to delineate passion or character. They possess these virtues by inheritance, not labor. They have complete control of themselves, while others who write to some purpose are but "stewards of their excellence" (the authors who gather up, use, and display effectively those qualities of life and character that constitute the true merit of all composition, and which never enter into the conceptions of these fastidious writers). They, like a summer flower, sweet while the summer lasts, live and die to themselves. If they attempt more than they can do, their writings, like that flower whose fragrance is changed by infection to a fetid odor, and less attractive than the ugliest weed, are unhealthy and demoralizing. As the odor of the lily in its decay is more offensive than the odor of the weed, so these writings, how beautiful soever they may seem, if tainted with falsehood, are worse in their effects than the unreliable works of scrubs and hacks.

Sonnet 95.

How sweet and lovely dost Thou make the shame
Which, like a canker in the fragrant rose,

Doth spot the beauty of Thy budding name!
O, in what sweets dost Thou Thy sins enclose!
That tongue that tells the story of Thy days,
Making lascivious comments on Thy sport,
Cannot dispraise but in a kind of praise;
Naming Thy name blesses an ill report.
O, what a mansion have those vices got
Which for their habitation chose out Thee,
Where beauty's veil doth cover every blot,
And all things turn to fair that eyes can see!
  Take heed, dear heart, of this large privilege;
  The hardest knife ill-us'd doth lose his edge.

In this stanza he tells us how effectually he has employed Truth in the delineation of error. In his dramas Truth has made error charming, by clothing the sins he depicted in attractive words. His lascivious scenes have been so naturally unfolded, that censure for their immoralities was disarmed by the admiration evoked by their beauty. The name of any of his characters was an excuse with the public for any sin it specially portrayed. Everything he has written has received the fullest public approval. This wonderful power is to be used with care, as by improper usage it will lose its effect.

Sonnet 96.

Some say Thy fault is youth, some wantonness;
Some say Thy grace is youth and gentle sport:
Both grace and faults are lov'd of more and less;
Thou mak'st faults graces that to Thee resort.
As on the finger of a throned queen
The basest jewel will be well esteem'd,
So are those errors that in Thee are seen
To truths translated, and for true things deem'd.

How many lambs might the stern wolf betray,
If like a lamb he could his looks translate!
How many gazers mightst Thou lead away,
If Thou wouldst use the strength of all Thy state!
But do not so; I love Thee in such sort,
As, Thou being Mine, Mine is Thy good report.

In this stanza he tells of the favorable welcome his dramas have received. Fault has been found by some with the licentious scenes he has written, but others have excused them as the product of youth and gayety. In both forms they have their admirers. He has been successful in converting faults into graces. As the worthless jewel on the finger of a powerful queen would be highly esteemed, so are the errors in his dramas, in the garb of Truth, received and adopted by the public as truth indeed. If the wolf could transform himself into the appearance of a lamb, it would add fearfully to his facilities for depredation. So if Thou (Truth) would give "the strength of all Thy state" (the name of Francis Bacon, instead of William Shakespeare, as the author of the dramas), he would add correspondingly to the number of his admirers. But this he must not do. His (Bacon's) love for "Thee" (his thoughts) is of a different sort. Thou (Truth) belongs to him as an author, and as the author (Shakespeare) only can he make report of his thoughts.

SONNET 97.

How like a winter hath My absence been
From Thee, the pleasure of the fleeting year!

> What freezings have I felt, what dark days seen,
> What old December's bareness everywhere!
> And yet this time remov'd was summer's time,
> The teeming autumn, big with rich increase,
> Bearing the wanton burthen of the prime,
> Like widow'd wombs after their lord's decease:
> Yet this abundant issue seem'd to me
> But hope of orphans and unfather'd fruit,
> For summer and his pleasures wait on Thee,
> And, Thou away, the very birds are mute;
> Or, if they sing, 't is with so dull a cheer
> That leaves look pale, dreading the winter's near.

He makes observations in this stanza upon the change in his life since he quit writing, and the increase and character of the poetry of others.

Since he left writing time has passed heavily. It has been like winter. He has been treated with coldness by friends, and at times driven almost to despair; has had no congenial occupation, and his surroundings imparted a gloom to his mind, which might be fitly compared to the nakedness of a December landscape. Yet it was summer time and succeeded by a "teeming autumn." Poets had been busy, and greatly increased their labors. The world around him was full of poesy, but much of it was anonymous, and some unfather'd (the work of fugitive writers). It had no charm for him. The time was desolate, which his old pursuit would have made delightful. Thou (Truth) was not with him, and he could not write. When he attempted to do so, his writings were dull, cold, and cheerless.

SONNET 98.

From You have I been absent in the spring,
When proud-pied April dress'd in all his trim
Hath put a spirit of youth in everything,
That heavy Saturn laugh'd and leap'd with him.
Yet nor the lays of birds nor the sweet smell
Of different flowers in odour and in hue,
Could make Me any summer's story tell,
Or from their proud lap pluck them where they grew;
Nor did I wonder at the lily's white,
Nor praise the deep vermilion in the rose:
They were but sweet, but figures of delight,
Drawn after You, You pattern of all those.
  Yet seem'd it winter still, and, You away,
  As with Your shadow I with these did play.

He tells in this stanza of the effect which the abandonment of Beauty has had upon his life.

The inspiration of Beauty, which, before he sought the appointment of solicitor, was so constant and delightful, though seemingly as inviting as ever, had no charm for him. Beauty's surroundings were fresh and spring-like. The same spirit animated him with youth; even the rest of Saturn was broken, and his mirth and jollity aroused. But neither the songs of birds nor the perfume of flowers could arouse in him the least ambition or desire to re-engage in writing. He had no story to tell, and was entirely indifferent to the different phases of beauty, which had once so charmed him. They seemed but pleasant objects to the sight,—forms in outline of his former joys. He felt that Beauty had forsaken him, and left only winter and gloom in his place.

The inference from this stanza, that while he is by preoccupation was prevented from giving any time to dramatic labor, other authors of the time were more busily employed than ever. He could see nothing in the beauty of their productions that was not imitative of his own. They did not attain to a full delineation of beauty as he had done, in particulars which he would proceed to illustrate in the next stanza.

SONNET 99.

The forward violet thus did I chide:
Sweet thief, whence didst thou steal Thy sweet that smells,
If not from My Love's breath? The purple pride
Which on Thy soft cheek for complexion dwells
In My Love's veins Thou hast too grossly dyed.
The lily I condemned for Thy hand,
And buds of marjoram had stolen Thy hair;
The roses fearfully on thorns did stand,
One blushing shame, another white despair;
A third, nor red nor white, had stolen of both,
And to this robbery had annex'd Thy breath;
But, for his theft, in pride of all his growth
A vengeful canker eat him up to death.
More flowers I noted, yet I none could see
But sweet or colour it had stolen from Thee.

He criticises the writings of contemporaries, and charges them with plagiarism.

One author, more conspicuous than the others, whom he calls the "forward violet," he charges with stealing so much of the truth as has given him reputation from the "breath" or fame of "My Love's breath" (his own works). He has also abused nature by the heightened color he has given to his characters,—comparing the hand to a "lily," and the hair to "buds of marjoram." His comparisons of shame and despair—roses standing on bushes bent with thorns—was false to nature, and the false mixing in coloring was so offensive, that it carried its own elements of decay with it. He could see nothing in the merit or beauty of other writers that had not been stolen from "Thee" (his thoughts).

SONNET 100.

Where art Thou, Muse, that Thou forget'st so long
To speak of that which gives Thee all Thy might?
Spend'st Thou Thy fury on some worthless song,
Dark'ning Thy power to lend base subjects light?
Return, forgetful Muse, and straight redeem
In gentle numbers time so idly spent;
Sing to the ear that doth Thy lays esteem
And gives Thy pen both skill and argument.
Rise, resty Muse, My Love's sweet face survey,
If Time have any wrinkle graven there;
If any, be a satire to decay,
And make Time's spoils despised everywhere.
Give My Love fame faster than Time wastes life;
So Thou prevent'st his scythe and crooked knife.

As if in disgust, he now calls upon Thou (Truth), as a muse, to redeem himself and renew his labor in that field where he as "Thy" (Thought) has won all his fame. Waste no more time in work that is of no value. Hide not your light in the obscurity of others; recall your powers and come back to me, and redeem the time you have wasted in noble labors. Sing for me (Bacon), who love thy poems, and give thee "skill and argument." Arouse yourself. Look at the work you once accomplished. Survey "My Love" (Lucrece), and satisfy yourself whether she has been injuriously affected by Time. If she has, it is for you to arrest her decay, and defeat the spoils of Time, by giving her universal renown. Multiply it faster than Time can destroy it, and defeat him in his cruel work.

SONNET 101.

O truant Muse, what shall be Thy amends
For Thy neglect of truth in beauty dyed?
Both truth and beauty on My Love depends;
So dost Thou too, and therein dignified.
Make answer, Muse, wilt Thou not haply say,
"Truth needs no colour, with his colour fix'd;
Beauty no pencil, beauty's truth to lay;
But best is best, if never intermix'd?"
Because he needs no praise, wilt Thou be dumb?
Excuse not silence so; for 't lies in Thee
To make him much outlive a gilded tomb,
And to be prais'd of ages yet to be.
  Then do Thy office, Muse; I teach Thee how
  To make him seem long hence as he shows now.

He charges his Muse with the offence of truancy, and asks what amends he will make to Thy (Thought) for neglecting "truth in beauty dyed" (to produce another poem like the former of "Venus and Adonis"), when truth and beauty have now only, My Love (Lucrece), as a dependence. Answer me, Muse! Thou (Truth) will probably say that Lucrece needs no change, and beauty needs no power to decorate her. They are both better for being separate. But, O Muse! will you be silent because truth needs no admiration, when it is in your power to give him immortal life, and cause him to be sought after and admired through all future time? Go to work at once under my instruction, and impart that life to Lucrece which shall give her that recognition in the future that she appears to have now.

SONNET 102.

My Love is strengthen'd, though more weak in seeming;
I love not less, though less the show appear:
That love is merchandiz'd whose rich esteeming
The owner's tongue doth publish everywhere.
Our love was new and then but in the spring
When I was wont to greet it with My lays,
As Philomel in summer's front doth sing
And stops her pipe in growth of riper days;
Not that the summer is less pleasant now
Than when her mournful hymns did hush the night,
But that wild music burthens every bough,
And sweets grown common lose their dear delight.
Therefore, like her, I sometimes hold My tongue,
Because I would not dull You with My song.

In this stanza he tells that he has commenced writing in verse.

He has recommenced writing, and finds that since he began to write this poem, his power, though seemingly weaker, is in fact greater. His theme affords him as much pleasure as his dramatic works, but will not be as generally appreciated. The works that command the admiration of the public are such as their authors wrote and sold to the theatres, or for general publication. His love for the poem at that time was new to him, in its spring-time, and like the whip-poor-will, who sings in the early summer, so he sang in verse when he began to write this poem. As she ceased with the advance of the year, so he, as years came, also ceased to write for a while. Not that he found less delight in the poem now than then, but the world was now full of the poetry of other writers, "wild music," and it had become so common as to lose its charm. For this reason he had been silent lest he should add to the dulness.

Sonnet 103.

Alack, what poverty My Muse brings forth,
That having such a scope to show her pride,
The argument, all bare, is of more worth
Than when it hath My added praise beside!
O, blame Me not, if I no more can write!
Look in your glass, and there appears a face
That overgoes My blunt invention quite,
Dulling My lines and doing Me disgrace.
Were it not sinful, then, striving to mend,
To mar the subject that before was well?
For to no other pass My verses tend
Than of Your graces and Your gifts to tell;
  And more, much more, than in My verse can sit
  Your own glass shows You when you look in it.

He speaks in this stanza of the difficulties which trouble him in recomposing the poem.

He can discover no improvement upon the version he had already written in his attempt to revise it. With a subject of unlimited range for display, the mere statement was better than the dress he gave it. He despairs of being able to finish it, and tells Beauty that the face she has formed for his heroine exceeds his powers of description, makes his lines tame, and shames his genius. Is it not wrong, then, to rewrite that which was so well told before, and thus disfigure the poem? His only aim is to delineate the charm and grace of his heroine, and beauty in those virtues is more highly adorned than he can depict him.

SONNET 104.

To Me, fair friend, You never can be old,
For as You were when first Your eye I eyed,
Such seems Your beauty still. Three winters cold
Have from the forests shook three summers' pride,
Three beauteous springs to yellow autumn turn'd
In process of the seasons have I seen,
Three April perfumes in three hot Junes burn'd,
Since first I saw You fresh, which yet are green.
Ah! yet doth beauty, like a dial-hand,
Steal from his figure, and no pace perceiv'd;
So Your sweet hue, which methinks still doth stand,
Hath motion, and Mine eye may be deceiv'd:
  For fear of which, hear this, Thou age unbred:
  Ere You were born was beauty's summer dead.

This stanza is addressed to Lucrece, his heroine, and tells when he first wrote the poem.

You (being the impersonation of Beauty) are

qualified in this stanza by the address "fair friend," at the commencement,—which means Lucrece. She can never be old to him, and is just as beautiful now as when he first wrote the poem. Three years have passed since that time, and she is still green, or fresh in his memory. As beauty steals from his figure with the imperceptible movement of the hand on the dial, so she, after so long a period, as he thinks, has life and movement; but lest he should be deceived, he will inform the poets, now so ambitious of renown, that "beauty's summer [was] dead" (was embodied in this poem) before they began to write.

SONNET 105.

Let not My love be call'd idolatry,
Nor My beloved as an idol show,
Since all alike My songs and praises be
To one, of one, still such, and ever so.
Kind is my love to-day, to-morrow kind,
Still constant in a wondrous excellence;
Therefore My verse to constancy confin'd,
One thing expressing, leaves out difference.
"Fair, kind, and true" is all My argument,
"Fair, kind, and true" varying to other words;
And in this change is my invention spent,
Three themes in one, which wondrous scope affords.
"Fair, kind, and true," have often liv'd alone,
Which three till now never kept seat in one.

His fondness for his own work, though great, must not be mistaken for idolatry, nor does he wish "My beloved" (Lucrece) to be admired beyond her deserts, as his object has been simply, in her character and conduct, to illustrate the influence of constancy. There was no change in her affection, and she remained true to her love, and emphasized the truthfulness of her life by self-inflicted death. This, to the exclusion of other thoughts, was the prominent feature of his poem. Her beauty, kindness, and truth, as changed only by words of like significance, had been the three themes which, though often separately considered, had never before in united form been portrayed in one poem.

The six stanzas commencing at 100 furnish a complete history of the poem of Lucrece. It was first written in 1591, but for some reason not published. Bacon says it was because the world was deluged with poetry at that time, and this poem, if published, would not be appreciated. The probability is that it was not in all respects finished to his liking, and he laid it by for further consideration. As this poem was written at the time that "Venus and Adonis" was published, we may presume that it was the "graver labor" to which he referred in the dedication of that "first heir of his invention" to the Earl of Southampton. This presumption finds confirmation in the fact that he did dedicate this poem to Southampton, when published in the following year, 1594.

These stanzas all refer to a recomposition of the poem, — a work which afforded him recreation during the long suspense of seventeen months, incurred by the delay of the queen in appointing a solicitor. If we may judge from his own words, this was the most distressing period of Bacon's early life. He had surrendered all congenial occupation to the exigency of the occasion. Those relatives who could have aided him treated him with coldness, and when, distrustful of them, he accepted the assistance of Essex, they, from pure jealousy of that nobleman, opposed him. Fear, anxiety, distrust, and suspicion by turns affected his mind. It is only by supposing that the labor he bestowed upon Lucrece at this time was in making a few changes, that we can account for the beauty and finish which adorns it.

Sonnet 106.

When in the chronicle of wasted time
I see descriptions of the fairest wights,
And beauty making beautiful old rhyme
In praise of ladies dead and lovely knights,
Then, in the blazon of sweet beauty's best,
Of hand, of foot, of lip, of eye, of brow,
I see their antique pen would have express'd
Even such a beauty as You master now.
So all their praises are but prophecies
Of this our time, all You prefiguring,
And, for they look'd but with divining eyes,
They had not skill enough Your worth to sing:
For we, which now behold these present days,
Have eyes to wonder, but lack tongues to praise.

On surveying the poems that have been written by former poets, he sees many descriptions of character, much beauty in the versification, and in the portrayal of the ladies and knights of the period represented. These same poets, so successful in that form of delineation, have also in the same form of verse attempted to give beauty a more life-like representation, in the personal charms of their female characters. They have sought to give expression to the same kind of character that he has since successfully delineated. Their attempts were but the forerunners of his success. They had the spirit of true poetry, but lacked the genius and skill. Their works excite our wonder, but we cannot praise them.

SONNET 107.

Not Mine own fears, nor the prophetic soul
Of the wide world dreaming on things to come,
Can yet the lease of My True Love control,
Suppos'd as forfeit to a confin'd doom.
The mortal moon hath her eclipse endur'd,
And the sad augurs mock their own presage;
In certainties now crown themselves assur'd,
And peace proclaims olives of endless age.
Now with the drops of this most balmy time
My Love looks fresh, and Death to Me subscribes,
Since, spite of him, I'll live in this poor rhyme,
While he insults o'er dull and speechless tribes;
And Thou in this shalt find Thy monument,
When tyrants' crests and tombs of brass are spent.

He has no longer any fear for his own safety, and there is nothing in the future to prevent him from returning to his dramatic labors, which he had supposed would be terminated by his appointment as solicitor. Queen Elizabeth, "the mortal moon," is dead, and James I., "the eclipse," has ascended the throne, and those who prophesied trouble and war were mistaken. All that was uncertain or doubtful in the future is now favorably settled, and peace promises to be enduring. The time is propitious for him; his dramas, which he supposed were completed, now seem to be renewed. They have lost no prestige, and will survive him. He will live in this poetic history, long after death has destroyed nations and peoples. And Thou (Truth) will have it for a memorial when kings and their tombs are decayed.

SONNET 108.

What's in the brain that ink may character
Which hath not figur'd to Thee My true spirit?
What's new to speak, what new to register,
That may express My Love or Thy dear merit?
Nothing, sweet boy; but yet, like prayers divine,
I must each day say o'er the very same,
Counting no old thing old, Thou mine, I Thine,
Even as when first I hallow'd Thy fair name.
So that eternal Love in Love's fresh case
Weighs not the dust and injury of age,
Nor gives to necessary wrinkles place,
But makes antiquity for aye his page,
  Finding the first conceit of love there bred
  Where time and outward form would show it dead.

His other self, Thee (his thoughts), is now recalled from his long exile, and questioned as to his ability to resume dramatic labor. Dŏ you need anything new? Has not he (Bacon) told you, as thought, all about his own powers? Is there anything new to speak or write about himself that you do not fully understand? Certainly not. He is essentially the same now that he was before their separation. His style of composition is as uniform as the prayers in the church service,—the same over and over, always fresh, never old. Thou (Truth) is his now as he is Truth's, just as he was when he first called Thy (Thought) to his aid. So that they may begin the composition of the new drama, just as if there had been no separation, and he had not grown older, but was following up the method he had first adopted. In that method he had made his first success, and to consult any other, depending upon time or external observation, would be to destroy their work.

SONNET 109.

O, never say that I was false of heart,
Though absence seem'd My flame to qualify.
As easy might I from Myself depart
As from My soul, which in Thy breast doth lie:
That is My home of love; if I have rang'd,
Like him that travels I return again,
Just to the time, not with the time exchang'd,
So that Myself bring water for My stain.
Never believe, though in My nature reign'd
All frailties that besiege all kinds of blood,
That it could so preposterously be stain'd,
To leave for nothing all Thy sum of good;
  For nothing this wide universe I call,
  Save Thou, My rose; in it Thou art My all.

Do not accuse him of inconstancy because, by absence, his work has been suspended. He could forsake "Myself" (Bacon as author) as easily as he could forsake "Thy" (Thought). In Thee is his real home, and if he has been away, like a traveller, he has returned as soon as he could, without any change that he has not repented of in tears, and "Myself" (Bacon as author) has returned with him. Don't believe, though he may be accused of all errors common to his race, that he would forsake Thou (Truth) for nothing; and as the universe would be nothing without Thou, so Thou (Truth) in the universe is his all.

SONNET 110.

Alas, 't is true I have gone here and there,
And made Myself a motley to the view,
Gor'd Mine own thoughts, sold cheap what is most dear,
Made old offences of affections new;
Most true it is that I have look'd on truth
Askance and strangely; but, by all above,
These blenches gave My heart another youth,
And worse *Essays* prov'd Thee My best of love.
Now all is done, have what shall have no end;
Mine appetite I never more will grind
On newer proof, to try an older friend,
A god in love, to whom I am confin'd.
Then give Me welcome, next My heaven the best,
Even to Thy pure and most most loving breast.

It is unfortunately true that, by the means he has used to obtain preferment, his life appears checkered to the world. He, "Myself" (as an author), has appeared in "motley" in theatrical representations. He has dissembled his thoughts, sold cheap his most precious works, offended old friends by his choice of new ones, and used deceit in avoidance of truth; but these errors, he calls heaven to witness, renewed in him the love which in his youth he had for contemplation and closet studies. The *Essays* which he wrote under that influence satisfied him that his dramas were his best performances. Now that they were finished, he would hereafter work upon the dramas, and never forsake them for other modes of composition. They were his idols, exclusive of all else. He besought Thy (his other self) to aid him with all his power, purity, and love, as next to heaven he was most dear to him.

Bacon's first appearance in his own name as an author, after his defeat, was in a small volume of "Essays," "Religious Meditations," and a table of "The Colors of Good and Evil." This was published in 1597, about two years after his defeat for the solicitorship. It doubtless contained the *Essays* to which he refers in this stanza ("and worse *Essays* prov'd Thee My best of love"), which proved that dramatic writing was better suited to his taste.

Sonnet 111.

O, for My sake do You with fortune chide,
The guilty goddess of My harmful deeds,
That did not better for My life provide
Than public means which public manners breeds.

Thence comes it that My name receives a brand,
And almost thence My nature is subdued
To what it works in, like the dyer's hand.
Pity me, then, and wish I were renew'd,
Whilst, like a willing patient, I will drink
Potions of eisel 'gainst My strong infection;
No bitterness that I will bitter think,
Nor double penance to correct correction.
  Pity me then, dear friend, and I assure Ye,
  Even that Your pity is enough to cure Me.

It will be observed in the line preceding the last that this and the following stanzas are addressed to "dear friend," a term which he uses to designate some one of his dramas or poems, as he used "fair friend" to designate Lucrece. The work here addressed is "Timon of Athens." This work in the folio of 1623 is classed as a tragedy. It was probably the first of his dramatic compositions after his defeat, and was intended allegorically to shadow his own bitter experience during the long struggle preceding that disaster.

The moral of the play is appealed to, to furnish an excuse for his own errors. He was educated for public life, taught to depend upon it for the means of life, instructed in those manners and usages which were to be observed by him on arriving to manhood. No other provision was made for him, nor did he know how else to conform to his condition in life. Extravagance in his expenses, display in his habit, profuseness in liberality, costly attendance, rich clothing,—all had involved him in debt. He had been required by his environments to live beyond his means, and all these misfortunes are fully delineated in the early life of Timon. As Timon was flattered, so was Bacon; as Timon was confiding, so was Bacon; as Timon was lavish of his means, so also was Bacon; and when they were exhausted, Timon found, as Bacon did, that those who professed the greatest love and honor for him in his day of prosperity, now deserted and opposed him in his efforts to repair his fortune. With this picture before him he exclaims, addressing the life he had written:—

> "O, for My sake do You with fortune chide,
> The guilty goddess of My harmful deeds,
> That did not better for My life provide
> Than public means which public manners breeds."

His life of indulgence exposed him to public reproach. He was branded for his extravagance and impecuniosity, and had once been arrested for debt, and spent a night in a sponging-house. Timon in similar circumstances had been driven to the wilderness. The unkindness which developed a perfect misanthropy and hatred in Timon, almost determined Bacon to abandon public pursuits, and adopt play-writing with its varied resources for a living. He sought consolation in the lesson he had furnished for himself in this play. That taught him submission, penitence, and composure.

SONNET 112.

Your love and pity doth the impression fill
Which vulgar scandal stamp'd upon My brow;
For what care I who calls Me well or ill,
So You o'er-green My bad, My good allow?
You are My all-the-world, and I must strive
To know My shames and praises from Your tongue;
None else to me, nor I to none alive,
That My steel'd sense or changes right or wrong.
In so profound abysm I throw all care
Of others' voices, that My adder's sense
To critic and to flatterer stopped are.
Mark how with My neglect I do dispense:
  You are so strongly in My purpose bred,
  That all the world besides methinks are dead.

The selfish love of Timon's flatterers, which was infinite in professions while he had money, and the wordy pity with which they refused him relief when his money was gone, fittingly portrayed how a similar experience had made Bacon a victim of common scandal and reproach. Like Timon, he had determined to disregard it entirely, and depict his virtues and vices, such as they were, in his dramas. He would know his shames and praises from them alone. Nothing else should determine for him the right from the wrong in his own life. As Timon went to the woods to escape the rebukes of his pretended friends, so he would hide his cares in a profound unconcern, for all that the world might say of him. He would be deaf alike to criticism and flattery, and by courting their neglect escape their deceit. The same philosophy which drove Timon to his death should make the world dead to him. This stanza is more fully interpreted in the note "Francis Bacon," following the poem.

SONNET 113.

Since I left You, Mine eye is in My mind,
And that which governs Me to go about
Doth part His function and is partly blind,
Seems seeing, but effectually is out;
For it no form delivers to the heart
Of bird, or flower, or shape, which it doth latch.
Of his quick objects hath the mind no part,
Nor his own vision holds what it doth catch;
For if it see the rud'st or gentlest sight,
The most sweet favour or deformed'st creature,
The mountain or the sea, the day or night,
The crow or dove, it shapes them to Your feature:
  Incapable of more, replete with You,
  My most true mind thus makes Mine eye untrue.

This stanza is the first addressed to You (Beauty) since he finished "Lucrece." He has been engaged since then in practical life, to the exclusion of the imagination, which, while it seems to see, is effectually blind. No impression is made by the objects of beauty which he beholds. None of the beauties of nature, birds, flowers, or shapes, awaken reflection. His mind is torpid concerning them, and his vision does not retain them. All sights, whether ugly, deformed, gentle, or sublime,—the sea, the day, the night, the crow, the dove,—are alike beautiful only, and that beauty in itself is replete. The most true mind, that which inspired him when he was writing, makes the mind which now governs him untrue in external observation.

SONNET 114.

Or whether doth My mind, being crown'd with You,
Drink up the monarch's plague, this flattery?
Or whether shall I say, Mine eye saith true,
And that Your love taught it this alchemy,
To make of monsters and things indigest
Such cherubims as Your sweet self resemble,
Creating every bad a perfect best,
As fast as objects to his beams assemble?
O, 't is the first; 't is flattery in My seeing,
And My great mind most kingly drinks it up:
Mine eye well knows what with his gust is greeing,
And to his palate doth prepare the cup;
If it be poison'd, 't is the lesser sin
That Mine eye loves it and doth first begin.

In this stanza he alludes to the tragedy of "King Lear." Referring to the preceding stanza, he is seemingly at a loss to determine whether it is the untruthfulness he attributes to the eye, or flattery, that has presented to his mind the subject of his tragedy. He is giving to monsters and "things indigest" (hurried and unnatural resolutions), the semblance of beauty,—Goneril and Regan, beautiful in form and feature, unlimited in the love they profess for their father, prove to be "monsters" of filial ingratitude. Edmund, the natural son of Gloster, personally attractive, is a "monster" of ingratitude, deceit, cruelty, selfishness, and treachery. These three characters are as perfectly bad as they can be made without violence to consistency. They are made to appear in their professions as perfectly good as possible, with like restriction. Lear, flattered by the professions of Goneril and Regan, and outraged by Cordelia's seeming remissness, gives everything to the former two, and disinherits and curses the latter. Gloster, deceived by Edmund, disowns Edgar, seeks to slay him, and loses his eyes through Edmund's treachery. The two fathers, by the flattery of their children, committed great errors through hastily formed (illy digested) resolutions. Thus the allusions in the stanza serve to identify the play.

Sonnet 115.

Those lines that I before have writ do lie,
Even those that said I could not love You dearer;
Yet then my judgment knew no reason why
My most full flame should afterwards burn clearer.
But reckoning Time, whose million'd accidents
Creep in 'twixt vows and change decrees of kings,
Tan sacred beauty, blunt the sharp'st intents,
Divert strong minds to the course of altering things,
Alas, why, fearing of Time's tyranny,
Might I not then say, "Now I love You best,"
When I was certain o'er incertainty,
Crowning the present, doubting of the rest?
Love is a babe; then might I not say so,
To give full growth to that which still doth grow?

In this stanza the progress of the tragedy reveals to the writer the falsity of what was before said in the 113th, about his love for beauty, though he did not foresee it at the time. Since then one of the million accidents of time has crept in to disturb the vows between parent and child (Gloster and Edgar), and has caused the king (Lear) to change his decrees. Cordelia's beauty, sacred in its truth and purity, could not avert her father's curse. His intentions were all blunted. His naturally strong mind was diverted from its original purpose, which was altered. In view of these occurrences, the writer, at the time he professed himself "replete with You" (Beauty), might have said with seeming truth, "Now I love You best." He was only mistaking Love in its infancy for Love in perfection, and making no allowance for its growth.

SONNET 116.

Let me not to the marriage of true minds
Admit impediments. Love is not love
Which alters when it alteration finds,
Or bends with the remover to remove:
O, no! it is an ever-fixed mark
That looks on tempests and is never shaken;
It is the star to every wandering bark,
Whose worths unknown, although his height be taken.
Love 's not Time's fool, though rosy lips and cheeks
Within his bending sickle's compass come;
Love alters not with his brief hours and weeks,
But bears it out even to the edge of doom.
If this be error and upon me prov'd,
I never writ, nor no man ever lov'd.

In this stanza the picture of Love is drawn from the lessons inculcated in the "Tempest." No impediments, however great, should separate honest men. Prospero's love for Antonio and Alonzo survived all wrongs they had inflicted upon him, though they removed him from his dukedom, and exposed him and his child to death. Their consciences, exhibited by a tempest which filled them with terror and dismay, and for a time brought desolation and grief to their hearts, also wrought repentance for their error, and restored them to happiness, bringing with it the blessing of a union through the loves of their children, stronger than ever. Thus was illustrated in the conduct of Prospero, the triumph of love over the power of revenge, and its survival after years of wrong and injury, while in the loves of Francisco and Miranda it was shown that the briefest love when mutual, where both are true, is only broken by death. If this be not true in morals, he has written in vain, and love has no existence.

Sonnet 117.

Accuse me thus: that I have scanted all
Wherein I should Your great deserts repay,
Forgot upon Your dearest love to call,
Whereto all bonds do tie Me day by day;
That I have frequent been with unknown minds,
And given to time Your own dear-purchas'd right;
That I have hoisted sail to all the winds
Which should transport Me farthest from Your sight.
Book both My wilfulness and errors down,
And on just proof surmise accumulate;

Bring Me within the level of Your frown,
But shoot not at Me in your waken'd hate;
Since My appeal says I did strive to prove
The CONSTANCY and VIRTUE of Your love.

In this stanza he applies the moral drawn from the "Tempest" to his own indifference to the claims of You (Beauty). He has been regardless of his deservings, forgotten all the delight beauty once afforded him, despite the unceasing dictates of his genius and inclination. He has engaged in pursuits in which beauty took no part, and sought various positions where he could never be seen. All this neglect he could be accused of, and it could be recorded against him. Nay, a thousand other errors, if just proof could be obtained, might increase this list to bring upon him the frown of beauty. But now that he had returned, and beauty had been aroused, he sought to avoid his anger, upon the plea that in Cordelia he had striven to prove the CONSTANCY, and in Miranda the VIRTUE, of beauty's love.

SONNET 118.

Like as, to make our appetites more keen,
With eager compounds We our palate urge,
As, to prevent our maladies unseen,
We sicken to shun sickness when we purge,
Even so, being full of Your ne'er-cloying sweetness,
To bitter sauces did I frame My feeding,
And, sick of welfare, found a kind of meetness
To be diseas'd, ere that there was true needing.

Thus policy in love, to anticipate
The ills that were not, grew to faults assur'd,
And brought to medicine a healthful state
Which, rank of goodness, would by ill be cur'd;
But thence I learn, and find the lesson true,
Drugs poison him that so fell sick of You.

As we use various compounds to sharpen the appetite, and medicines which sicken us to avoid real sickness, so he, enraptured with beauty, turned his attention to less congenial occupation, which, while it did not disturb his life, was unsuited to his wishes. This change in his life, not necessary at the time, had the effect of weaning him from his studies, and involving him in all the tricks and arts of a seeker for office. He had had enough of this experience, and had learned from it, that while it had injured his name, it had only increased his love for the cherished pursuits he had left.

SONNET 119.

What potions have I drunk of Siren tears,
Distill'd from limbecks foul as hell within,
Applying fears to hopes, and hopes to fears,
Still losing when I saw Myself to win!
What wretched errors hath My heart committed,
Whilst it hath thought itself so blessed never!
How have Mine eyes out of their spheres been fitted
In the distraction of this madding fever!
O benefit of ill! now I find true,
That better is by evil still made better;
And ruin'd love, when it is built anew,
Grows fairer than at first, more strong, far greater.
So I return rebuk'd to My content,
And gain by ill thrice more than I have spent.

In this stanza he tells how the change in his life had affected him.

He had been deceived and allured by the false promises and insincere professions of pretended friends. At one moment his hopes were bright and clear, while the next they were darkened with fear. He was certain of success to-day, to-morrow as certain of defeat. He had been misled by his hopes, in his calculations, when he thought success assured. The care, anxiety, and unceasing labor of the contest had unfitted him for literary work. This terrible experience had, in comparison, added new charms to his old pursuits. He could engage in them anew with more delight. The works he would produce would be fairer, stronger, and greater. Rebuked as he had been by forsaking, he would be content in returning to them, and thus gain by his experience thrice more than he had paid for it.

Sonnet 120.

That You were once unkind befriends me now,
And for that sorrow which I then did feel
Needs must I under My transgression bow,
Unless my nerves were brass or hammer'd steel.
For if you were by My unkindness shaken
As I by Yours, You 've pass'd a hell of time,
And I, a tyrant, have no leisure taken
To weigh how once I suffer'd in your crime.
O, that our night of woe might have remember'd
My deepest sense, how hard true sorrow hits,

And soon to You, as You to Me, then tender'd
The humble salve which wounded bosoms fits!
But that Your trespass now becomes a fee;
Mine ransoms Yours, and Yours must ransom Me.

He refers back to the time of the discovery of his own lines in the drama of another, mentioned in the eighty-sixth stanza, as marking the unkindness of Beauty, and the immediate cause of their long separation. All his sorrow and transgression had occurred since then. So greatly had they affected him, that only nerves of brass or steel would be unshaken by them. If Beauty had been similarly affected during the same period, the time must have been infernal in torment. He had taken no leisure to estimate it, but if on that night that he made the discovery he could have known the trials and afflictions that he had since experienced, he would never have surrendered Beauty for the struggles of an office-seeker. Now that he had come back, Beauty's trespass upon his powers was in the nature of a fee, and they must mutually forgive each other.

Sonnet 121.

'Tis better to be vile than vile esteem'd,
When not to be receives reproach of being,
And the just pleasure lost which is so deem'd
Not by our feeling, but by others' seeing;
For why should others' false adulterate eyes
Give salutation to my sportive blood?
Or on My frailties why are frailer spies,
Which in their wills count bad what I think good?

No, I am that I am, and they that level
At My abuses reckon up their own:
I may be straight, though they themselves be bevel;
By their rank thoughts my deeds must not be shown;
Unless this general evil they maintain,
All men are bad, and in their badness reign.

He thinks it preferable to be really guilty of the plagiarisms with which he has been charged, than, being not guilty, to suffer the reproach, as in the latter case, knowing his own merit, he is deprived of the public appreciation, and suffers unjustly. Why should other writers, who are more guilty than he of using the writings of others to dress up their wit, be his accusers? Why should those who have made licentiousness the subject of their dramas charge him with it, and denounce as wicked what he thinks good? He obeys his own taste in his works, and asks no favors of those around him. They only publish their own guilt in the effort to blacken him. For aught they know, he may be right and they wrong. Neither the truth nor falsity of his writings must be tried by what they may ignorantly say of them, unless they assume ignorance and pretension to be proper standards of judgment for all men to adopt.

Sonnet 122.

Thy gift, Thy tables, are within My brain
Full character'd with lasting memory,
Which shall above that *idle rank* remain
Beyond all date, even to eternity;

Or at the least, so long as brain and heart
Have faculty by nature to subsist;
Till each to raz'd oblivion yield his part
Of Thee, Thy record never can be miss'd.
That poor retention could not so much hold,
Nor need I tallies Thy dear love to score;
Therefore to give them from me was I bold,
To trust those tables that receive Thee more:
  To keep an adjunct to remember Thee
  Were to import forgetfulness in me.

His power as a writer and all the resources he has employed are born of himself. They can never be lost to him, and are equally inaccessible to his ignorant accusers. They will endure forever, or at least as long as brain and heart subsist. Until these are destroyed they will remain. His manuscripts could not contain them, and as he needed nothing to remind him of them, he had destroyed all records, trusting to the table of his memory which had received them in their full development. It would be a reproach to his memory to keep any mementos of the work which he held in such loving veneration.

It may be fairly inferred from the two preceding stanzas, that the plays which appeared in Shakespeare's name had aroused the envy of contemporaneous writers. They sought to depreciate them in the public estimation by charging the author with plagiarism. He replies by accusing them with an aggravated use of the same means, and the additional charge of ignorance, which disqualifies them from judging him correctly. But lest their charges should at some time be substantiated by his papers and memoranda, he destroys them all, trusting to his memory, and claims his works as the product of his own brain.

SONNET 123.

No, Time, Thou shalt not boast that I do change:
Thy pyramids built up with newer might,
To Me are nothing novel, nothing strange;
They are but dressings of a former sight.
Our dates are brief, and therefore we admire
What Thou dost foist upon us that is old,
And rather make them born to our desire,
Than think that we before have heard them told.
Thy registers and Thee I both defy,
Not wondering at the present nor the past,
For Thy records and what we see doth lie,
Made more or less by Thy continual haste.
This I do vow and this shall ever be:
I will be true, despite Thy scythe and Thee.

In this stanza he apologizes for, or rather excuses, any use he may have made of the works of former writers in the construction of his own.

Time can know no change in him, as there is nothing new in the past. No description of the pyramids, however animated or glowing, could make them appear novel or strange to him. It would be but a new description of what he had known before. Our lives are short, and rather than spend them in search of new wonders, we admire the old ones, and each observer, led by his own tastes, finds new beauties in them that he has never heard mentioned by others. He would not trust to the records that all ages have furnished of things in the past or present, for his own opinon of them; because they depend upon the accounts which, being formed from both careful and careless examination, are necessarily untrue. But in his writings, also founded upon events and stories of past ages, he will write truly, despite all the changes of time. Such truth as they afford in the illustration of truth, philosophy, poetry, character, and life, he will use, without regard to the skeleton which the past has furnished to be decorated by them. In this respect his dramas differ from those of his contemporaries, who are satisfied to use the stories and events of the past, as of themselves sufficient for their work.

SONNET 124.

If My dear love were but the child of state,
It might for Fortune's bastard be unfather'd,
As subject to Time's love or to Time's hate,
Weeds **among** weeds, or **flowers** with flowers gather'd.
No, it was builded far from accident;
It suffers not in smiling **pomp, nor falls**
Under the blow of thralled discontent,
Whereto the inviting time **our fashion calls:**
It fears not policy, that heretic,
Which works on leases of short-number'd hours,
But all alone stands hugely politic,
That it nor grows with heat nor drowns with showers.
To this I witness call the fools of time,
Which die for goodness, who have liv'd **for crime.**

In this stanza he contrasts the permanency of his writings with the character he has drawn of Posthumus in the play of "Cymbeline," which he was probably composing at the time. Posthumus was the adopted child of Cymbeline, and was subject to such fortune as Time held in store for him, whether good or bad,—a weed among weeds, or a flower among flowers. So his play, if it were similarly exposed, would suffer from similar causes. But this was not its fortune. Unlike Posthumus, it was unaffected by accident, owed nothing to the pomp and glitter of the court, and free of obligation, suffered nothing from the unkindness of majesty as Posthumus did. It suffered from no policy that, as in the case of Posthumus, limited his stay at court at the risk of his life. But it was a creation of itself, defiant of all the elements of court life and power. Those courtiers who spent their lives in dancing attendance upon majesty, and were finally rewarded with frowns, disappointments, and often death itself, would do well to profit by such an example. (See note "Francis Bacon," for further interpretation.)

Sonnet 125.

Were 't aught to me I bore the canopy,
With my extern the outward honouring,
Or laid great bases for eternity,
Which prove more short than waste or ruining?
Have I not seen dwellers on form and favour
Lose all, and more, by paying too much rent,

For compound sweet foregoing simple savour,
Pitiful thrivers, in their gazing spent?
No, let Me be obsequious in Thy heart,
And take Thou my oblation, poor but free,
Which is not mix'd with seconds, knows no art,
But mutual render, only Me for Thee.
Hence, thou suborn'd informer! a true soul
When most impeach'd stands least in thy control.

Of what value was it to him that he bore the canopy of royalty, and with his presence honored the outward show? How did it aid him to labor for long months to attain favor from the queen, which eventuated in the waste of fortune and disappointment of his hopes? Had he not seen others deceived in the same way, who for the allurements of office gave up honest life, and spent their all for preferment? No; he was satisfied with the delights of authorship, with delineating truth in character, which, while affording no wealth, is free of care, and a source of constant enjoyment. It placed him beyond the reach of informers, and preserved his integrity of purpose and life.

SONNET 126.

O Thou, My lovely boy, who in Thy power
Dost hold Time's fickle glass his fickle hour;
Who hast by waning grown, and therein show'st
Thy lovers withering as Thy sweet self grow'st;
If Nature, sovereign mistress over wrack,
As Thou goest onwards, still will pluck Thee back,
She keeps Thee to this purpose, that her skill
May time disgrace and wretched minutes kill.

Yet fear her, O Thou minion of her pleasure!
She may detain, but not still keep, her treasure;
Her audit, though delay'd, answer'd must be,
And her quietus is to render Thee.

This stanza refers entirely to "Hamlet." The irresolution of the prince in avenging the murder of his father is alluded to in the "fickle glass and fickle hour" of time, as being held by Thou (Truth) for his own purpose. This hesitation, or "waning," of Hamlet has grown, and become a more prominent feature of his character as time advanced. It has shown the "lovers withering" in the separation of Hamlet and Ophelia, and her death. Nature, despite the wreck of his mind and hopes, and the love he bore to his mother, still withheld him from his purpose, that the disgrace of his mother by her hasty marriage with Claudius might be clearly illustrated, and due preparation made for the "wretched minutes" in which all were slain. Although held back and detained, Thou (Truth) had a further motive, the death of Hamlet himself, whom he detained, that he might skilfully arrange for that denouement, "and her [Nature's] quietus is to render Thee." (See note "Francis Bacon," for further interpretation.)

Commentators generally believe that the 127th Sonnet is the beginning of a new series, which conveys a meaning entirely distinct from anything contained in the preceding Sonnets. I have before me, while writing this, a photo-lithographic fac-simile of the first quarto edition of the Sonnets of 1609, "from the copy in the British Museum, by Charles Praetorius, Photographer to the British Museum," etc. In the space between the 126th and 127th Sonnets two pairs of parenthetical characters occur, thus (were they put there by the artist?):—

(·)
(   )

They are seeming reproductions of the printed work. Why are they there? They occur at the close of the first stanza in which allusion is made to Hamlet (126), and preceding the first in which Othello is indicated (127). This last stanza is followed by one (128) ludicrously descriptive of the attempts of other authors to imitate the spirit and style of the dramas, and that by one (129) which suggests the guilty love of Claudius and Gertrude in "Hamlet." A ludicrous description of "My Mistress" (Tragedy.), indirectly alluding to Othello, occurs in 130.

The parenthetical characters have some significance. They would hardly be selected to designate the commencement of a new series; but as suggestive of the omission or tranposition of two stanzas, their appearance is both natural and proper. If two approximate stanzas could be found that would restore the breaks in the sequence of the poem, would it not be reasonable to conclude that they belonged in the spaces inclosed by the parentheses? Place 129 after 126, and follow the last with 128, and the breaks in both Hamlet and Othello are repaired, and the description of each is uninterrupted. This is the only instance in the entire poem where the meaning is clouded by transposition. It is so marked that it ought to assure the genuineness of the discovery which completes the thought.

SONNET 127.

In the old age black was not counted fair,
Or if it were, it bore not beauty's name;
But now is black beauty's successive heir,
And beauty slander'd with a bastard shame:
For since each hand hath put on nature's power,
Fairing the foul with art's false borrow'd face,
Sweet beauty hath **no name,** no holy bower,
But is profan'd, **if not lives in** disgrace.
Therefore My Mistress' brows are raven black,
Her eyes so suited, and they mourners seem
At such who, not born fair, no beauty **lack,**
Sland'ring creation with **a** false esteem;
  Yet so they mourn, becoming of **their woe,**
  That every tongue says beauty should look so.

Othello is the drama signified in this stanza. Until the present time, white people only have been represented in the leading characters of the dramas. Black is now selected for that purpose, and Beauty is represented in Desdemona as suffering from the foulest slander that can assail a wife. As the other writers of the age have attempted to delineate nature in tragic illustration of life, and made artificial work of it, Beauty has no place, or name, or protection in their writings. He is profaned and disgraced by them. For the purpose of rescuing him, having chosen Tragedy for his Mistress, he now presents him in black. His observation will be employed to demonstrate in his work that personal beauty is not necessarily the only beauty, and the world may be deceived by it. In the anguish and distress of Othello he will depict a beauty that shall be admired by all.

Thence to the close of the poem, it is supposed to be addressed to his Mistress, and many strange and curious opinions as to what manner of person she must have been, to answer the description given her by the poet, have been sanctioned by the best Shakespearian scholars of all generations since the poem appeared. She was of very dark complexion, of a fiery nature, passionate beyond all reason, false in all the elements of good character, and, as the author has written, in general make-up a perfect devil. That Shakespeare should have loved such a woman, and published the fact to the world, has given birth to deeper regrets and weaker apologies than any similar sin ever received. If these writers had by chance lit upon the idea that Bacon instead of Shakespeare was the author of this poem, with the knowledge which history gives of his life and character, I am prone to believe they would have sought and found a more pleasing and satisfactory interpretation than the one so generally adopted.

Let us suppose, then, as I have attempted to prove, that in the 126 stanzas preceding this one, Lord Bacon has told us, in allegory, of the manner in which these plays were produced, and given many good reasons why, not wishing to be known as their author, he had disposed of the authorship to Shakespeare. Let us accept as true what he tells us, that he found his highest delight in composing them, that by forsaking that employment to engage in office-seeking and politics, he brought shame and disgrace upon his name, and unending sorrow to his life. His only source of relief was to re-engage in the work which had afforded him so much happiness. He had found that in the attempt to do so, his powers were stronger than ever, his inclinations and tastes had not been changed, and that his strong desire was to enter upon a new field of investigation, which should represent character and life in the intensest modes of crime and passion. It is this change in the aspect of the plays he is now writing that he foreshadows in "My Mistress." It is Tragedy. He has written Comedies and Histories, but in this mightier field, he has never entered. The public taste is favorable. Tragedy was not popular when he wrote his first plays, and the little tragedy they contained "bore not Beauty's name" (gave to Tragedy no distinctive character; they were known only as Comedies or Histories). Now, however, it was in favor; it "was Beauty's successive heir." A host of dramatists, Marlow, Lodge, Jonson, and others, were at work upon tragedies, but their portrayal of character was untrue to nature; they faired "the foul [the darkest characters] with art's false borrow'd face," and thus profaned and disgraced Beauty. For this, among other good reasons, he had made choice of Tragedy.

SONNET 128.

How oft, when Thou, my music, music play'st,
Upon that blessed wood whose motion sounds
With Thy sweet fingers, when Thou gently sway'st
The wiry concord that Mine ear confounds,
Do I envy those jacks that nimble leap
To kiss the tender inward of Thy hand,
Whilst My poor lips, which should that harvest reap,
At the wood's boldness by Thee blushing stand!
To be so tickled, they would change their state
And situation with those dancing chips,
O'er whom Thy fingers walk with gentle gait,
Making dead wood more bless'd than living lips.
  Since saucy jacks so happy are in this,
  Give them Thy fingers, Me, Thy lips to kiss.

He tells us in this stanza of the amusement it affords him to witness the vain efforts and struggles of other writers, to imitate and rival him in the delineation of Truth in his dramas. Their efforts are likened to the exercise of the fingers when playing upon the virginals. The virginals represent the progress of literary work. Thou, or Truth, is supposed to be the inspirer of the work in hand, in the production of which he uses the fingers of Thy, the thinker or creator, and the jacks or keys to the instrument are the authors themselves. The music, or the matter which the instrument thus formed produces, "confounds" him. He would like the opportunity to try his skill, and see if he could not excel those writers. If he could be as well pleased with his own efforts as they seem to be with theirs, he would gladly exchange places with them and produce better work. But as they, "the saucy jacks," are so well satisfied, let them work on with the fingers, or slight touches of truth. He will receive it from the lips, the only reliable source.

Sonnet 129.

The expense of spirit in a waste of shame
Is lust in action; and till action, lust
Is perjur'd, murtherous, bloody, full of blame,
Savage, extreme, rude, cruel, not to trust,
Enjoy'd no sooner but despised straight,
Past reason hunted, and no sooner had
Past reason hated, as a swallow'd bait
On purpose laid to make the taker mad;
Mad in pursuit and in possession so;
Had, having, and in quest to have, extreme;
A bliss in proof, and prov'd, a very woe;
Before, a joy propos'd; behind, a dream.
All this the world well knows; yet none knows well
To shun the heaven that leads men to this hell.

This stanza, which describes the guilty passion that influenced Claudius to murder his brother, and led to all the grief, sorrow, death, and final destruction of the characters delineated in Hamlet, tells its own story better than any interpretation.

Sonnet 130.

My mistress' eyes are nothing like the sun;
Coral is far more red than her lips' red;
If snow be white, why then her breasts are dun;
If hairs be wires, black wires grow on her head.
I have seen roses damask'd, red and white,
But no such roses see I in her cheeks;
And in some perfumes is there more delight
Than in the breath that from My mistress reeks.
I love to hear her speak, yet well I know
That music hath a far more pleasing sound;
I grant I never saw a goddess go;
My mistress, when she walks, treads on the ground:
  And yet, by heaven, I think My Love as rare
  As any she belied with false compare.

In this stanza the falsities used by contemporaneous writers to describe feminine attractions are ingeniously travestied by the negative accomplishments of his Mistress. Her eyes are unlike the sun. Coral is redder than her lips. If nothing is white but snow, her breasts are dun. If hairs are wires, black wires grow on her head. He has never seen any damask roses in her cheeks, and has smelled perfumes that are sweeter than her breath. Music is more pleasing to his ear than her voice. He has never seen a goddess move, but his Mistress walks on the ground like other people; and yet "My Love" (the drama) is as rare and beautiful as any woman whose beauties have been belied by false comparisons, none of which could add a single grace to her person.

SONNET 131.

Thou art as tyrannous, so as Thou art,
As those whose beauties proudly make them cruel;
For well Thou know'st, to My dear doting heart
Thou art the fairest and most precious jewel.
Yet, in good faith, some say that Thee behold,
Thy face hath not the power to make love groan:
To say they err I dare not be so bold,
Although I swear it to Myself alone.
And, to be sure that is not false I swear,
A thousand groans, but thinking on Thy face,
One on another's neck, do witness bear,
Thy black is fairest in My judgment's place.
In nothing art Thou black save in Thy deeds,
And thence this slander, as I think, proceeds.

His picture of Thou (Truth) and Thy (Thought), as delineated in the character of Othello, is referred to in this stanza. Othello in his jealous rage is as tyrannical in conduct as others of fairer mould would be. He is in his view the most perfect of all the characters of his creation. But many will pronounce him unnatural, and think him unfitted to represent the character of a lover. He will not publicly deny this opinion, but in his own mind, "Myself" (as author), he is certain it is wrong, and to make sure of that, he will fill the play with pathetic scenes illustrating the noble qualities of the Moor, and a thousand vices, which he will display in the character of Iago. They prove to him that Othello will be much the best and fairest character, as he is only black in his deed of slaying Desdemona. The slander or censure of the drama will probably be attributable to that scene.

SONNET 132.

Thine eyes I love, and they, as pitying me,
Knowing Thy heart torments Me with disdain,
Have put on black and loving mourners be,
Looking with pretty ruth upon My pain;
And truly not the morning sun of heaven
Better becomes the grey cheeks of the East,
Nor that full star that ushers in the even
Doth half that glory to the sober West,
As those two mourning eyes become Thy face.
O, let it then as well beseem Thy heart
To mourn for Me, since mourning doth Thee grace,
And suit Thy pity like in every part!
Then will I swear beauty herself is black,
And all they foul that Thy complexion lack.

He is perplexed to know how to reconcile his subject with truth in its delineation. The character of the Moor almost surpasses his power. His thoughts are so varied that they aggravate him, and the complexion he has chosen for Othello, as well as the subject, presents many difficulties. But as a theme it is full of attractions for him; he sees it only in the light of truth and beauty, and if he can properly portray the pathetic parts of the drama, as he can see them in the several characters, the play will excel all others that he has ever written. Othello has been often pronounced the masterpiece of Shakespeare. We here see that opinion confirmed by the author himself, and learn, also, that he encountered greater difficulty in composing it than in any other of the great dramas.

SONNET 133.

Beshrew ***that heart*** that makes **My heart** to groan
For that deep wound it gives My friend and Me!
Is 't not enough **to** torture Me alone,
But slave to slavery My sweet'st friend must be?
Me from Myself Thy cruel eye hath taken,
And My next self Thou harder hast engross'd:
Of Him, **Myself, and** Thee, I am forsaken;
A torment thrice threefold thus to be cross'd.
Prison My heart in Thy steel bosom's **ward,**
But then My Friend's heart let My poor heart bail;
Whoe'er keeps Me, let My heart be his guard;
Thou canst not then use rigor in My gaol:
  And yet Thou **wilt; for I,** being pent in Thee,
  Perforce am Thine, and all that is in **Me.**

In the forty-fifth stanza the poet tells us that his life is made of four. The allusion is to the four characters of the Key,—I, meaning himself (Bacon), Thou (Truth), Thy (Thought), and You (Beauty). In order to comprehend clearly the details of the transfer which he makes to Shakespeare, in this and the three following stanzas, it will be necessary to observe these parts of what he calls his life, as separate impersonations, and to apply the distinctive appellation of each to the changes in form belonging to it; thus, I, My, Mine, Me, signifies Bacon; Thou, Thine, Truth; Thy, Thee, Thyself, Thought; You, Yours, Yourself, Beauty; Myself means Bacon as author; My Friend means Shakespeare. This explanation is repeated here for the convenience of the reader.

The subtilety of meaning conveyed in the four following stanzas, the abruptness of the changes, and the compactness of expression require the closest attention to enable the reader to comprehend their true object. There is ample verge in all of them for cavil. They describe a complete abandonment of the dramas by Bacon in favor of Shakespeare.

"That heart," which he refers to as making his "heart to groan," is his own heart filled with fear, anxiety, care, and suspicion, lest by some treachery, accident, design, or oversight, he will be exposed as the author of the dramas. Influenced by these fears, the demands of public office, and his speculative and philosophical studies, he has determined to abandon dramatic composition. His revenue from public sources amply supplies his wants. His prospects for advancement are flattering. He has been knighted, and ranks foremost among the courtiers and statesmen of the age. He is the confidant and adviser of the king. Delightful as the recreation has always been to delineate nature, truth, and beauty in character, it has ceased to be of use to him as a pursuit, is an encroachment upon his time, and an inspirer of his fears. Yet the thought of forsaking it causes his other "heart to groan." That other heart ("my heart") is his regret at parting forever with the fruit of those mighty labors, which, as he says, have ever been his "best of love," and for which he has so often predicted an assured immortality. While he lives he can never be known as their author. It would be ruinous to all his hopes, possibly fatal to his life. His heart groans at the thought, and is deeply wounded.

He feigns to consider Shakespeare a sufferer from the same "deep wound." "Is 't not enough to torture Me alone," he asks, "but slave to slavery my sweet'st friend must be?" How Shakespeare becomes the "slave to slavery" will appear from a statement of the facts derived from the Sonnets. Thou (Truth), Thy (Thought), and You (Beauty) are the creators of these dramas. I (Bacon), have been your instrument or slave in producing them. Shakespeare is my instrument or slave in assuming the authorship of them. Therefore I being the slave of Thou, Thy, and You, and Shakespeare being my slave, he is the "slave to slavery."

He tells in the accusation of Thy (Thought), in the next line, what is meant by the inquiry: "Is 't not enough to torture Me alone?" "Me" he says, "from Myself Thy cruel eye hath taken," that is, Bacon in person is separated from Bacon in authorship. His works, which reflect his real self, can never, while he lives, be known as his.

"And my next self," he continues in allusion to Shakespeare, "thou harder hast engross'd." In plainer phrase, by consenting to be known as the author, Shakespeare is "engross'd" or convicted by Thou (Truth) of falsehood or living a lie. The conclusion is arrived at in the next line, "Of him (Shakespeare), Myself (my works), and Thee, (Thought), I (Bacon) am forsaken." This he declares to be "a torment thrice threefold thus to be cross'd." This may be explained thus: the first threefold refers to *Him* (Shakespeare), Him, He, His; the second to *Myself* (my works), Myself, Mine, My; the third, *Thee* (Thought), Thee, Thy, Thyself. This makes the thrice threefold torment, as all those have forsaken him.

Having thus made the transfer, he proceeds to give directions for his own concealment: "Prison My heart in Thy steel bosom's ward"; as if saying to himself: "Let me be careful to secrete in my own thoughts all knowledge of the origin of these dramas." "But then My Friend's [Shakespeare's] heart let My *poor* heart bail." Let "My *poor* heart" (the entire works) be sufficient, with Shakespeare's name as author, for his protection. "Whoe'er keeps Me, let My heart be his guard." Whatever change of condition may occur in my life, let my heart (my knowledge of the authorship of the dramas) still be concealed as the guard of Shakespeare. "Thou canst not then use rigor in My gaol." By pursuing this course the truth will never be known, and nothing can occur to make such revelation necessary. "And yet Thou wilt; for I, being pent in Thee, perforce am Thine, and all that is in Me." This is simply a foil to the reader. Of course Thou (Truth) will tell him of it, because "perforce" it is in "Thee," his thoughts.

Sonnet 134.

So, now I have confess'd that he is Thine,
And I Myself am mortgag'd to Thy Will,
Myself I'll forfeit, so that other Mine
Thou wilt restore, to be My comfort still:
But Thou wilt not, nor he will not be free,
For Thou are covetous and he is kind;
He leard'd but surety-like to write for Me
Under that bond that him as fast doth bind.
The statute of Thy beauty Thou wilt take,
Thou usurer, that put'st forth all to use,
And sue a friend came debtor for My sake;
So him I lose through My unkind abuse.
Him have I lost; Thou hast both him and Me:
He pays the whole, and yet am I not free.

In this stanza he follows up the transfer with an allusion to his confession, as he terms it, in the preceding stanza, that Shakespeare is Thou's, not that Thou is Shakespeare's. "And I myself am mortgag'd to Thy WILL." He has given the authorship of his works (Myself) to "Will," and personally (I), has mortgaged his "heart" as a "guard" against exposing the transaction. "Myself I'll forfeit so that other Mine [Shakespeare] Thou wilt restore to be My comfort still." He will forfeit the works, if Thou wilt restore Shakespeare to him, with the revenue that he has been in the habit of receiving from him. But Thou, who is "covetous," and Shakespeare, who is kind to Thou, will not do it, and Shakespeare is not "free" or willing to pay any longer. This closes the assignment, and Shakespeare becomes thereby the owner as well as recognized author of the dramas.

He tells us in the next two lines how Shakespeare first became interested with him in the dramas. "He learn'd but *surety-like* to write for Me under that bond that him as fast doth bind." Under a bond of mutual confidence and sworn secrecy, Shakespeare "learn'd" from Bacon that he, upon certain conditions, was to become Bacon's "surety" against exposure as the author of the dramas, by assuming the authorship himself. This announcement makes the agreement between them complete, for we have seen in previous stanzas that Shakespeare was recognized as the author; that Bacon received part of the proceeds; that the agreement was to close at Bacon's option; and from these stanzas under consideration, we learn that Bacon abandons both authorship and compensation, and gives all to Shakespeare.

The untruth or falsity of Shakespeare, in thus permitting his name to be used as author, is punished by Thou (Truth), who, by virtue of Thy's (Thought's) statute of Beauty, which is but another name for the dramas, sues and convicts Shakespeare on the bond which he made with Bacon. Bacon loses him because of the part he has persuaded him to act ("through my unkind abuse"), and Shakespeare as Bacon's surety is held responsible to Thou (Truth) for the ownership and authorship of the dramas ("he pays the whole"), yet Bacon is liable to suspicion and exposure ("yet am I not free").

SONNET 135.

Whoever hath her wish, Thou hast Thy Will,
And Will to boot, and Will in overplus;
More than enough am I that vex Thee still,
To Thy sweet will making addition thus.
Wilt Thou, whose will is large and spacious,
Not once vouchsafe to hide My will in thine?
Shall will in others seem right gracious,
And in My will no fair acceptance shine?
The sea, all water, yet receives rain still
And in abundance addeth to his store;
So Thou, being rich in Will, add to thy Will
One will of Mine, to make Thy large Will more.
Let no unkind, no fair beseechers kill;
Think all but one, and Me in that one Will.

He tells Thou (Truth) in this stanza that he has obtained possession of "Thy [Thought's] will" (the entire works) and "Will to boot" (Shakespeare), and of "will in overplus" (his own (Bacon's) will), of which last will he says: "More than enough am I that vex Thee [Thought] still, to Thy sweet will [thy works] making addition thus."

With the fear of exposure constantly before him, he now invokes Thou's aid. "Wilt Thou, whose will is large and spacious, not once vouchsafe to *hide* My will in Thine?" If I am suspected, and search should be made in the works for evidence to implicate me, let them not find it in any of the truths I may have written. Like the rain, which is undistinguishable from the sea when it falls into it, so let my will be undistinguishable from thine. Add my will to the will of Thy, and thus increase thy large "Will" (Shakespeare). Let no unkind ones (enemies to me), "no fair beseechers [no smooth, cunning courtiers] kill" (destroy my prospects, and drive me into obscurity). Think of the dramas, of me, and of Shakespeare as all one, and all known as "Will" (Shakespeare).

SONNET 136.

If Thy soul check Thee that I come so near,
Swear to Thy blind soul that I was Thy Will,
And Will, Thy soul knows, is admitted there;
Thus far for love my love-suit, sweet, fulfil.
Will will fulfil the treasure of Thy love,
I fill it full with wills, and My will one.
In things of great receipt with ease we prove
Among a number one is reckon'd none:

> Then in the number let Me pass untold,
> Though in Thy store's account I one must be;
> For nothing hold Me, so it please Thee hold
> That nothing Me, a something sweet to Thee:
> Make but My name Thy love, and love that still,
> And then Thou lov'st me, — for My name is Will.

Pursuing the request for protection, he in this stanza addresses Thy (Thought), "If Thy soul" (thy love of truth) "check Thee that I come so near" (that I ask you thus to suppress the truth), "swear to Thy blind soul" (tacitly or outwardly acknowledge) "that I was thy Will; Thy soul" (thy love of truth) "knows Will" (Shakespeare) "is admitted there" (to thy blind soul). Do this for love of me.

This request is followed by the assurance "Will [Shakespeare] will fulfil the treasure of Thy love." What was the treasure of Thy love? In the twentieth stanza, where the description of Thou (Truth) is given, the poet, after investing Thou with every virtue, closes by saying: "Mine be Thy love, and Thy love's use their treasure" (Thy love be my love, and the product of that love its treasure). In plainer phrase, the dramas I have composed are Thy love, and these Shakespeare now owns and "will fulfil" (manage) as he pleases. I (Bacon) fill that "treasure" full of wills, and my will one. That "treasure," composed of all the characters delineated in the dramas, each representing a single will, are his, and my will is among them. It is my will they should be thus disposed of.

He now tells Shakespeare that "in things of great receipt," one is very easily proved to be none. Therefore, in the great number of wills you have received, and which you are to claim as your own, "let my will pass untold" (don't mention or breathe it, but consider it as nothing). If it please Thee (Thought) hold "that nothing as something sweet to Thee." As he (Bacon) must be one in Thy store's account, Thy (Thought) can make his name of Bacon his love, "and love that *still*" (love it in quiet, alone, by Thyself). If Thy will do that, then he will love him by his other name that he has chosen,—the name of "Will" (as provided at the close of the last and the beginning of this stanza).

In the quarto of 1609 the sixth line of this Sonnet reads: "I fill it full of wills." Commentators have changed this reading to "Ay, fill it full of wills." This latter version makes Shakespeare instead of Bacon "fill it full of wills." "I" is undoubtedly correct.

Why should the writer of these four stanzas have used so much ingenuity in disclosing a simple transaction, if not that it might sooner or later inform the world that he was the true author of the dramas? He has foreshadowed in a hundred lines of this poem the immortal name they would win for their author; but the requirements of his position denied him that fame during his own life. Posthumous fame was all he could anticipate, and for this he prepared by concealing the true history of the dramas, under a key in this poem, and leaving it "to foreign nations and the next ages."

The fame and renown which Bacon sought for his personal enjoyment, he expected to realize from the high positions he filled in public life. His philosophy was for posterity. He knew that would give enduring life to his memory. In a letter to the Bishop of Winchester, after his fall, he says:—

"As for my essays and some other particulars of that nature, I count them but as the recreation of my other studies, and in that sort I propose to continue them, though I am not ignorant that those writings would, with less pain and embracement, perhaps, yield more lustre and reputation to my name than those which I have in hand; but I count the use that a man should seek of the publishing of his own writings before his death to be but an untimely anticipation of that which is proper to follow a man, and not go along with him."

As if supplementary to this thought, we find in his will the following strikingly prophetic passage: "My name and memory I leave to men's charitable speeches, foreign nations, and the next ages." His avowed works gave no occasion for these utterances. They had passed the ordeal of public scrutiny, and in them his name and memory were immortal. He knew there was something more, trusted to time, which future ages in the light of these Sonnets might reveal; but when that revelation would be made, and whether in his own or some foreign nation, was hid from his view, and he left it for time to disclose. If it were not so, and he really had no desire that future generations should know him as the writer of these immortal dramas, why did he write the Sonnets? As a mere riddle for posterity to solve, they have thus far only served to puzzle the brains of all writers and readers, and stain the memory of their imputed author. Viewed in any other light than that in which the Key unfolds them, they defy all efforts to give them coherency, dignity, or even decency; but with this Key to their meaning, they become a marvellous history, and most impressive appeal to the world for justice to the memory of one of the greatest benefactors of our race. It was with the belief that sooner or later they would be deciphered, that he wrote the transfer to Shakespeare in this and the three preceding Sonnets. It is noticeable that throughout the Sonnets the poet wraps every passage containing a fact in language or imagery of either joyful or passionate import. He never tires of expressing his wonder and delight at the power of You (Beauty), or his grave, thoughtful, and loving appreciation of Thou (Truth). How tender and parental is his regard for "My Love" (his dramas) and how frequent and assuring to the three are his promises of immortality. "My Mistress" (his tragedies), the dearest portion of his dramas, he endows with passions, crimes, and cunning, illustrative of predominating traits in character. If he supposes a difficulty in composition, he charges it to Thou, You, or himself. All his disclosures are only to be made through the strangest and most ingenious compound of imagery, metaphor, allegory, and narrative.

SONNET 137.

Thou blind fool, Love, what dost Thou to Mine eyes,
That they behold, and see not what they see?
They know what beauty is, see where it lies,
Yet what the **best** is take the worst to be.
If eyes corrupt **by** over-partial looks
Be anchored in **the bay** where all men ride,
Why of eyes' falsehood hast Thou forged hooks,
Whereto the judgment of My heart is tied?
Why should My heart think that a several plot
Which My heart knows the wide world's common place?
Or Mine eyes, seeing this, say this **is not,**
To put fair truth upon so foul a face?
In things right true My **heart and eyes** have err'd,
And to this false plague are they now transferr'd.

In this stanza he describes the jealousy with which he intends to invest Othello, by a number of questions addressed to Love, which he charges with having led him away from the truth. Why, in the beauty and simplicity of Desdemona, does he not see her as he did at first? He knows she is beautiful in her person, but that which he most loved, her pure and virtuous character, now appears vile and depraved. So long as men are naturally tempted by the personal charms of feminine beauty and complaisance, wherever seen, why should he make that common attraction the subject of his work? Why should the plot he is developing appear singular to him, when he knows it is one of the ordinary affairs of life? Why, seeing that, should he say to himself, that truth in character is entirely incompatible with this conduct in beauty? His observation and reflection are both at fault.

Sonnet 138.

When My Love swears that she is made of truth,
I do believe her, though I **know** she lies,
That she might think Me some untutor'd youth,
Unlearned in the world's false subtleties.
Thus vainly thinking that she thinks Me young,
Although **she knows My** days are past the best,
Simply **I** credit her false-speaking tongue;
On both sides thus is simple truth suppress'd.
But wherefore says she not she is unjust?
And wherefore say not I that I am **old?**
O, love's best habit is in seeming trust,
And age in love loves not to have years told;
Therefore I **lie** with her and **she with** me,
And in our faults by lies we flatter'd be.

He thinks he has followed truth and nature in the delineation of jealousy, yet done great violence to truth in the characterization of the drama (My

Love). The drama might convey the impression that he is ignorant of human nature, or that, though past middle life, he is too young, too fresh in his knowledge of the deceits and subtleties of life, to depict the passion of jealousy truly. He will submit to that opinion, but adhere to his plan. If that is a mistake, he will love it all the same, and the dramas will exhibit his fault, but not rob him of his pleasure. The falsehoods he creates will best represent the faults of his characters.

SONNET 139.

O, call not Me to justify the wrong
That Thy unkindness lays upon My heart;
Wound Me not with Thine eye, but with Thy tongue;
Use power with power, and slay Me not by art.
Tell Me Thou lov'st elsewhere, but in My sight,
Dear heart, forbear to glance Thine eye aside;
What need'st Thou wound with cunning when Thy might
Is more than My o'er-press'd defence can bide?
Let Me excuse Thee: ah! my Love well knows
Her pretty looks have been Mine enemies,
And therefore from My face she turns My foes,
That they elsewhere might dart their injuries;
  Yet do not so, but since I am near slain,
  Kill Me outright with looks and rid My pain.

He will not justify the wrong with which his thoughts of human misery and distress have filled his heart. Thou (Truth), instead of blaming him, and using art and trickery to dissuade him from his work, should convince him by argument, "use power with power." If Thou's view differ from his, yet Thou must stand by him and give him true counsel, and no cunningly devised expedients, for he is perplexed to know how to reconcile his thoughts with truth in the progress of the work. All the beauty and interest he has given to the love of Othello is now changed to jealousy and hate, and will end in murder. The difficulty of depicting this in character he is prone to think surpasses his skill.

Sonnet 140.

Be wise as Thou art cruel; do not press
My tongue-tied patience with too much disdain,
Lest sorrow lend me words, and words express
The manner of My pity-wanting pain.
If I might teach Thee wit, better it were,
Though not to love, yet, Love, to tell me so,
As testy sick men, when their deaths be near,
No news but health from their physicians know;
For if I should despair, I should grow mad,
And in My madness might speak ill of Thee:
Now this ill-wresting world is grown so bad,
Mad slanderers by mad ears believed be.
  That I may not be so, nor Thou belied,
  Bear Thine eyes straight, though Thy proud heart go wide.

In this stanza he determines the limit which he will give to Othello's grief, by causing Desdemona to give him the proper advice. It is as if one actor representing Desdemona was advising the representative of Othello. She says to him: "Don't overact and make yourself too offensive in your charges and epithets. Such a course would make my part, which is remarkable for mildness and submission, untrue. To make it correspond to your severe reproof, unqualified by love, it would be natural for me in my extremity of sorrow to betray in words all that part of the charge against me which, by being concealed, is the strongest feature in the drama. My idea is, that you should affect love for me to the last. As men when near death hear nothing but encouragement from their physicians, so should it appear that, with a cruel death near, I am not unloved by my slayer. Without this it would be natural for me in my despair to make charges against you (Othello), and the audience by believing them would lose the charm of the play. That this may not occur, nor truth be belied, don't deviate from a truthful delineation, whatever your thoughts may be."

Sonnet 141.

In faith, I do not love Thee with Mine eyes,
For they in Thee a thousand errors note;
But 't is My heart that loves what they despise,
Who in despite of view is pleas'd to dote;
Nor are Mine ears with Thy tongue's tune delighted,
Nor tender feeling, to base touches prone,
Nor taste, nor smell, desire to be invited
To any sensual feast with Thee alone:
But My five wits nor My five senses can
Dissuade one foolish heart from serving Thee,
Who leaves unsway'd the likeness of a man,
Thy proud heart's slave and vassal wretch to be;
  Only My plague thus far I count My gain,
  That she that makes Me sin awards Me pain.

The errors, crimes, and vices that he has depicted in Othello are not what he admires. It is the picture they present to his heart. His love for that is the love of a dotard. The words have no charm for his ear, nor is he attracted by the tender feeling of Othello transformed into jealousy. No sensual feeling is aroused by the beauty of the Tragedy, but neither his wits nor his senses can turn his thoughts from the man they have created. He sees in him the pure nobility of nature transformed by jealousy into a slave and demon, and in Desdemona a lovely woman, a triumph in portrayal, grossly belied and foully murdered.

SONNET 142.

Love is My sin and Thy dear virtue hate,
Hate of My sin, grounded on sinful loving:
O, but with Mine compare Thou Thine own state,
And Thou shalt find it merits not reproving;
Or, if it do, not from those lips of Thine,
That have profan'd their scarlet ornaments
And seal'd false bonds of love as oft as Mine,
Robb'd others' beds' revenues of their rents.
Be it lawful I love Thee, as Thou lov'st Those
Whom Thine eyes woo as Mine importune Thee;
Root pity in Thy heart, that when it grows
Thy pity may deserve to pitied be.
If Thou dost seek to have what Thou dost hide,
By self-example may'st Thou be denied!

He has in this Tragedy striven to show how a pure and unstained love, between husband and wife, may be ruined by hate inspired by the husband's jealousy, and end in the destruction of both. And Thou (Truth), as guilty as himself in making false vows, breaking marital ties, and violating nuptial faith, has no reason to reprove his work. He has not violated Truth more than Thou (Truth) himself has violated it in the thoughts he has portrayed, which, though harsh, have been alleviated by pity; and that pity has in its turn wrought pity for Othello's misery. If Truth seeks to reveal what he has kept concealed, the real truth of the purity of Desdemona, and the cause of Othello's jealousy, prematurely, his own example should restrain him.

Sonnet 143.

Lo! as a cheerful housewife runs to catch
One of her feather'd creatures broke away,
Sets down her babe, and makes all swift dispatch
In pursuit of the thing she would have stay,
Whilst her neglected child holds her in chase,
Cries to catch her whose busy care is bent
To follow that which flies before her face,
Not prizing her poor infant's discontent;
So run'st Thou after that which flies from Thee,
Whilst I, Thy babe, chase Thee afar behind:
But if Thou catch Thy hope, turn back to Me,
And play the mother's part, kiss me, be kind;
So will I pray that Thou may'st have Thy Will,
If Thou turn back, and My loud crying still.

The closing scene of Othello perplexed the author with the idea that he had not been entirely true to nature in the delineation of character. He illustrates the doubt by a figure. Thou (Truth), the superintending genius of all his writings, is likened to a careful housewife, who is regardful of all matters appertaining to the household. Her babe bears the same relation to her that the author of Othello bears to Thou. The doubt is illustrated by the chicken that has escaped. Thou (Truth), who forsakes the author, like the mother who leaves her child to reclaim the chicken, is in hot pursuit after the doubt. The author, like the babe, loudly crying, follows Thee (his own thoughts) far behind. Which is right? This is the question. Thee (his own thoughts) suggests that the scene will be more effective if worked up slowly, but Thou (Truth) thinks it should be rapid. Should Othello, in his anger, hate, and jealousy, have slain Desdemona on the instant, after being convinced of her guilt? or was it natural for him to wait, and do it deliberately after his passion had cooled? Truth favors the former view, and would satisfy the doubt at once, but the author selects the latter, and is represented as crying for truth to return; in other words, by arousing pity for Othello, he makes the scene conformable to nature, and thus "Thy Will" (Shakespeare, the imputed author, the only author known to the world) is reinstated in Thou's favor.

Sonnet 144.

Two loves I have of comfort and despair,
Which like two spirits do suggest Me still;
The better angel is a man right fair,
The worser spirit a woman color'd ill.

To win Me soon to hell, My female evil
Tempteth My better angel from My side,
And would corrupt My saint to be a devil,
Wooing his purity with her foul pride.
And whether that My angel be turn'd fiend
Suspect I may, yet not directly tell;
But being both from Me, both to each friend,
I guess one angel in another's hell:
  Yet this shall I ne'er know, but live in doubt,
  Till My bad angel fire My good one out.

The two angels in this stanza are Macbeth and his wife. Macbeth is the "better angel," and Lady Macbeth the "woman color'd ill." Lady Macbeth is the tempter. By her influence Macbeth is corrupted and led into crime. The natural goodness of his nature is overcome by her pride and strength of character, and the evil ambition of both. The Tragedy is not advanced sufficiently to enable the author to forecast the fate of Macbeth. He suspects what it may be, but is yet uncertain. As the creation is his own, and the two angels are friends, he guesses that one is enmeshed in the toils of the other. Of this, however, he will not be positive until the tragedy is completed.

Sonnet 145.

Those lips that Love's own hand did make
Breathed forth the sound that said "I hate"
To Me that languish'd for her sake;
But when she saw My woeful state,
Straight in her heart did mercy come,
Chiding that tongue that ever sweet

Was us'd in giving gentle doom,
And taught it thus anew to greet.
"I hate" she altered with an end,
That follow'd it as gentle day
Doth follow night, who like a fiend
From heaven to hell is flown away;
"I hate" from hate away she threw,
And sav'd My life, saying "not you."

The hatred excited by the crimes of Macbeth and his wife is portrayed by the whisper of Love in his (the author's) ear of the words "I hate," in the midst of his work. She is moved with pity at the sight of woe and horror he is depicting. Having been kind and gentle on former visits when he was writing, she greets him anew with the same words in milder tone, which dispels all dread of her displeasure when he hears the qualification, "not you." Being exonerated, his "life" (Macbeth) is saved, and the tragedy continued.

Sonnet 146.

Poor soul, the centre of My sinful earth,
Press'd by these rebel powers that Thee array,
Why dost Thou pine within and suffer dearth,
Painting Thy outward walls so costly gay?
Why so large cost, having so short a lease,
Dost Thou upon Thy fading mansion spend?
Shall worms, inheritors of this excess,
Eat up Thy charge? is this Thy body's end?
Then, soul, live Thou upon Thy servant's loss,
And let that pine to aggravate Thy store;
Buy terms divine in selling hours of dross;
Within be fed, without be rich no more:
So shalt Thou feed on Death, that feeds on men,
And Death once dead, there 's no more dying then.

The literal meaning of the first line of this stanza is, "Macbeth, the central figure in my tragedy." He is represented at that stage of the drama where his castle is invested by the army of Malcolm and Macduff. He is suffering within from fear, and making a show of ability to resist, by the display of his banners on the outward walls. This show and bravado will avail nothing, and the thought of death and its consequences afflicts him. Aggravated by his servant's report of the enemy's force, he gathers fresh courage by recalling the "terms divine,"—the promise of the witches that he need not fear till Birnam Wood do come to Dunsinane, and that he should not yield to one of woman born (the previous promises of the same witches, foretelling his greatness, which had been confirmed). He ceases to have faith in human power, and relies entirely upon the witches' prophecy, which he deems of divine origin. He slays young Siward, which strengthens his faith in his invulnerability. The picture is the same as the one more fully detailed in the tragedy.

Sonnet 147.

My Love is as a fever, longing still
For that which longer nurseth the disease,
Feeding on that which doth preserve the ill,
The uncertain sickly appetite to please.
My reason, the physician to My Love,
Angry that his prescriptions are not kept,
Hath left Me, and I desperate now approve,
Desire is death, which physic did except.

Past cure I am, now reason is past care,
And frantic-mad with evermore unrest;
My thoughts and My discourse as madmen's are,
At random from the truth vainly express'd;
For I have sworn Thee fair and thought Thee bright,
Who art as black as hell, as dark as night.

His Love (the Tragedy) is yet in progress. The death of Lady Macbeth must furnish some counterpoise to the crimes that have stained her life. He likens his Love (the Tragedy) to a fever still in progress, feeding upon all the disturbances which aggravate its intensity. He is depicting Lady Macbeth. Her reason has fled. Her physician can be of no service, death, which defies medicine, being near. She is frantic for want of rest. She talks madly of her life, referring in random expressions to her foul and bloody crimes. Without exciting some pity for her in the audience that witness the performance, nothing can make her realize the personal attractions of beauty and intellect with which he intended to endow her. She will be only black in crime and dark in delirium, without sympathy, and detested for her infamy.

Sonnet 148.

O Me, what eyes hath love put in My head,
Which have no correspondence with true sight!
Or, if they have, where is My judgment fled,
That censures falsely what they see aright?
If that be fair whereon My false eyes dote,
What means the world to say it is not so?

If it be not, then Love doth well denote
Love's eye is not so true as all men's no.
How can it? O, how can love's eye be true,
That is so vex'd with watching and with tears?
No marvel then, though I mistake My view;
The sun itself sees not till heaven clears.
  O cunning Love! with tears Thou keep'st Me blind,
  Lest eyes well-seeing Thy foul faults should find.

The self-criticism is continued. In this stanza he contrasts the criminality of the character he has drawn in Macbeth with truth. There is no correspondence between them. His judgment condemns the crimes of Macbeth and his wife, yet he delights in portraying them. Why should the world condemn them? If he is infatuated, then Love is untrue, and the world is right. How can that Love be true which is exhibited in delirium and tears? It will not surprise him if he is in error. The sun sees not the earth till the heavens are clear, so he will not see his error until his work is done. He will be blind to the faults of Lady Macbeth, and depict her delirium and watching lest the world see her infamy only.

Sonnet 149.

Canst Thou, O cruel, say I love Thee not,
When I against Myself with Thee partake?
Do I not think on Thee, when I forgot
Am of Myself, all tyrant, for Thy sake?
Who hateth Thee that I do call My friend?
On whom frown'st Thou that I do fawn upon?
Nay, if Thou lower'st on Me, do I not spend
Revenge upon Myself with present moan?

What merit do I in Myself respect,
That is so proud thy service to despise,
When all My best doth worship Thy defect,
Commanded by the motion of Thine eyes?
  But, love, hate on, for now I know Thy mind;
  Those that can see Thou lov'st, and I am blind.

In this stanza all the allusions point to the tragedy of Antony and Cleopatra. Substitute Antony and Cleopatra for the writer, and Thee as the interlocutors in the stanza, and the conversation would assume a form after this manner: Antony asks Cleopatra: "How can you be so cruel as to say I do not love you, when, against all the teaching of my better nature, I partake with you in sin? Do I not forget myself in thinking of you and giving you all my affections? Who hates you that is my friend? Whom do you hate that I love? When you chide me, am I not submissive to your will? Have I any merit of renown that is not devoted to your service, while thus infatuated with your personal charms and power?" He represents this condition of the leading characters as the limit of disclosure in the tragedy, and himself blind as to what will follow.

Sonnet 150.

O, from what power hast Thou this powerful might
With insufficiency My heart to sway?
To make Me give the lie to My true sight,
And swear that brightness doth not grace the day?
Whence hast Thou this becoming of things ill,
That in the very refuse of Thy deeds

There is such strength and warrantise of skill
That, in My mind, Thy worst all best exceeds?
Who taught Thee how to make Me love Thee more
The more I hear and see just cause of hate?
O, though I love what others do abhor,
With others Thou shouldst not abhor My state;
 If Thy unworthiness rais'd love in Me,
 More worthy I to be belov'd of Thee.

The conversation between the writer and Thee in this stanza, resumed, as a fresh appeal of Antony to Cleopatra, would reproduce the thoughts expressed between them in similar form. "Whence do you get this power to sway my heart with insufficiency, and cause me to belie my own convictions of truth? Why make me swear that your Egyptian face is more beautiful than one of fairer hue? Why is it that you have power to make evil so attractive that your worst acts in my eyes exceed the best? Who taught you how to make me love you more, the more I see just cause to hate you? My countrymen abhor me, and would deprive me of my renown for loving you; but you should not join with them in that hatred, nor should you repel me from you, because I am enamored of your personal charms."

Sonnet 151.

Love is too young to know what conscience is;
Yet who knows not conscience is born of love?
Then, gentle cheater, urge not My amiss,
Lest guilty of My faults Thy sweet self prove;
For, Thou betraying me, I do betray
My nobler part to My gross body's treason;

My soul doth tell My body that he may
Triumph in love; flesh stays no farther reason;
But, rising at Thy name, doth point out Thee
As his triumphant prize. Proud of this pride,
He is contented Thy poor drudge to be,
To stand in Thy affairs, fall by Thy side.
  No want of conscience hold it that I call
  Her "love" for whose dear love I rise and fall.

Continuing the address to Cleopatra in this stanza, Antony pleads that his love for her is too fresh, too strong, to be under any conscientious restraint. Yet who knows but conscience is born of love, and if so, why should you remind me of having violated it, when you, my ideal of love, may prove guilty of a like offence. When Truth (Thou) forsakes me, my body controls all my nobler qualities, and my soul resigns my body to uncontrolled sensual indulgence. I need no other license for the enjoyment of that love I bear for you. It is that which makes me your drudge and slave. For that I have forsaken wife, home, country, and the honor and renown of a great life, conscience and all, to aid in the affairs of your kingdom, and "fall by your side."

Sonnet 152.

In loving Thee Thou know'st I am forsworn,
But Thou art twice forsworn, to Me love swearing,
In act Thy bed-vow broke and new faith torn,
In vowing new hate after new love bearing.
But why of two oaths' breach do I accuse Thee,
When I break twenty? I am perjur'd most;

For all My vows are oaths but to misuse Thee,
And all My honest faith in Thee is lost:
For I have sworn deep oaths of Thy deep kindness,
Oaths of Thy love, Thy truth, Thy constancy,
And, to enlighten Thee, gave eyes to blindness,
Or made them swear against the thing they see;
For I have sworn Thee fair; more perjur'd I,
To swear against the truth so foul a lie!

In this stanza, pursuing the same form of address to Thou and Thee, he gives Cleopatra's reply to Antony. "You know I am forsworn in loving you, as I am the widow of Ptolemy; but you are twice forsworn in swearing love to me.—once to Fulvia, who died after your first visit here, and now to Octavia, to whom you are just married. Your bed-vow to Octavia is broken, and the new faith you have given her violated, by thus disregarding your marital ties. But I am wrong to accuse you of breaking two oaths, when I break twenty. I am the worst criminal, for all my vows lead to the misdirection of your great qualities. I have lost all honest faith in you, because you have proved false to the kindness that I credited you with, as well as to the love, truth, and constancy which I believed I enjoyed in your attentions. I made myself blind to your falsities, and would not see them because I felt certain of your great love for me. I was truly perjured in swearing this against the truth, as since revealed in your perfidy."

SONNET 153.

Cupid laid by his brand, and fell asleep:
A maid of Dian's this advantage found,
And his love-kindling fire did quickly steep
In a cold valley-fountain of that ground;
Which borrow'd from this holy fire of love
A dateless lively heat, still to endure,
And grew a seething bath, which yet men prove
Against strange maladies a sovereign cure.
But at My Mistress' eye Love's brand new-fir'd,
The boy for trial needs would touch My breast;
I, sick withal, the help of bath desir'd,
And thither hied, a sad distemper'd guest,
  But found no cure: the bath for My help lies
  Where Cupid got new fire, — My Mistress' eyes.

SONNET 154.

The little Love-god lying once asleep
Laid by his side his heart-inflaming brand,
Whilst many nymphs that vow'd chaste life to keep
Came tripping by; but in her maiden hand
The fairest votary took up that fire
Which many legions of true hearts had warm'd,
And so the general of hot desire
Was sleeping by a virgin hand disarm'd.
This brand she quenched in a cool well by,
Which from Love's fire took heat perpetual,
Growing a bath and healthful remedy
For men diseas'd; but I, My Mistress' thrall,
  Came there for cure, and this by that I prove,
  Love's fire heats water, water cools not love.

These two stanzas, the last a reproduction in sentiment of the first, simply state the fact that the god of Love provided, in a spring or well, water that would prove a sovereign cure for "strange maladies." In order to test it, he caused the writer, who wished to find some remedy for the incessant influence he was under to display life in character, in Tragedy, to go there and bathe. He found no cure.

The bath for his help lies "where Cupid got new fire,—My Mistress' [Tragedy] eyes."

FRANCIS BACON.

Lord Campbell says of Bacon's writings: "Of all the compositions in any language I am acquainted with, these will bear to be the oftenest perused, and after every perusal they still present some new meaning and some new beauty." The same observation will apply with broader significance to his life. As often as it has been written, each new biographer has revealed new phases in his character, which relieves it of some of its repulsive features. That he committed great errors, cannot, in the light of his own confessions, be denied; but many of his acts represented as criminal and corrupt take their complexion from the age in which we live, no allowance being made for the laws, customs, habits of life and thought that prevailed during the reigns of Elizabeth and James. Bacon, judged by his contemporaries, was no worse than they; but it was his fortune, whether good or bad, to be more conspicuous by reason of his wonderful genius and prolific pen. Viewed in the light of intellectual achievement, he was the most remarkable man of modern times. If

Greece or Rome ever produced his superior, their histories fail to record it. What he would have accomplished for humanity, if his early hopes and designs had not been thwarted by the death of his father, and the consequent loss of his patrimony, it is impossible to conceive; but that he would have escaped the errors and mistakes of the life he was obliged to adopt, there can be but little doubt, — for, though educated for public life, his tastes, inclinations, and intentions were all at that time wedded to speculative and philosophical pursuits.

It is painfully apparent from his letters to his uncle, Lord Burleigh, begging for some more congenial employment, that it was with a heavy heart that he entered Gray's Inn to fit himself for the profession of the law. Slender means and expensive tastes soon involved him in debt. He became the prey of the money sharks of the time, was arrested, and spent a night in a sponging-house. This experience, coupled with the natural longing of his nature for that indulgence of taste and curiosity to which he had been accustomed, doubtless suggested the idea of merchandising his thoughts as a means of supplying his purse. When this thought occurred to him, or at what time he began to write his dramas, must be left to conjecture. He entered Gray's Inn in 1580, at the age of twenty. Shakespeare, who was to figure as his coadjutor, came to London from Stratford in 1585 or 1586. It was probably after this latter event that he sought for means to put his scheme in execution. One great obstacle must have presented itself. He was the son of a nobleman who had filled the highest offices in the realm, and the nephew of Lord Burleigh, the queen's great prime minister. The profession he had chosen must in a few years introduce him into the duties and responsibilities of official public life. All his hopes and opportunities for preferment and renown depended upon success in his profession. Next to proficiency in that, nothing was of more importance than a character formed after the models furnished in the lives and conduct of the successful men of the time. He plainly foresaw that to be known as a playwright would blast all his hopes, and assign him to a position among a class to whom all worthy social privileges and chances for favorable recognition were hopelessly denied. How to avoid such a fate, and make his scheme successful, must have given him much anxiety.

I am more than inclined to believe that as a recreation to the study of the law, he had, previous to this time, written the comedy of "Love's Labor 's Lost," and gave it that suggestive title to signify that the hours of pleasure spent in composing it were wasted, and of no account. The many beautiful passages it contained, its fertile imagery, and philosophical speculations, were to him like the revelation of a new world. They made him familiar with his own powers. As compared with the dramas of the time, this one was vastly superior. How he would delight to see it performed! Previous to this time he had participated in masques and plays as an amateur, whenever any festival or public occasion offered at Gray's Inn. We may suppose that by this and similar appeals to his glowing fancy, the subject grew in importance, and gave him little rest until he had devised a plan for its presentation at Blackfriars. He had learned by frequent attendance at the theatre how to please an audience. Much circumspection and entire secrecy must be observed to make his plan successful, but some one must be trusted. Should he succeed, he would be able, not only to supply "this consumption of the purse," but to delight in witnessing his own drama. Unquestionably many schemes were devised and abandoned before he concluded to trust William Shakespeare. And why was he selected? We look into the history of the times for an answer. The name of playwright in those days was but another name for a man of vicious and abandoned life. Green, one of the best, died a wretched drunkard and *debauchee.* Marlow, next to Shakespeare in rank as a writer, was slain in a drunken brawl. So of many others; and where all were bad, it was no easy task to find one who could be trusted. Shakespeare had not been contaminated by the vices of his associates. He came to London in the pursuit of fortune, possibly to escape the consequences of some wild freak of his youth. His life at Stratford had not been free from stain. He had been charged with poaching. He was forced into an early and ill-assorted marriage, and had left his native town under a cloud. Despite these blots, he was the only man in theatrical life in whose simplicity, deportment, and general bearing Bacon saw that he could venture to confide. At great risk, he made choice of him, unbosomed his purpose to him, and found an ardent and trustworthy co-worker, who from that moment became, in effect, the author of the great works which ever since have borne his name.

Strong bonds of mutual confidence were entered into between them. It was understood by both that whenever Bacon, from prudential or other motives, should cease to write, Shakespeare should retain his assumed authorship of the plays, and enjoy the avails. Until that time, they were to share alike in the profits. Addressing Thy (Thought) in the thirty-seventh Sonnet, he says:—

> "So then I am not lame, poor, nor despis'd,
> Whilst that this shadow doth such substance give
> That I in Thy abundance am suffic'd
> And by a *part* of all Thy glory live."

The merit of his own productions, apparent to him at first, made his work a labor of love; more to be preferred than "public honor or proud titles." He never tires in this poem of assuring it the immortality it has since enjoyed.

From a passage in Green's "Groatesworth of Wit," it is quite certain that Shakespeare posed as a playwright prior to 1592, and with Bacon's aid contributed somewhat to the composition of two historical dramas,—one called the "True History of the Contention between the Houses of York and Lancaster," the other, "The True Tragedy of Richard Duke of York." These plays were afterwards incorporated into the second and third parts of Henry VI., which was first published in the folio of 1623, seven years after Shakespeare's death. He was not publicly known as a dramatist until several of the plays, which afterwards bore his name, had been often performed at Blackfriars. "Venus and Adonis," a poem which in the dedication to the Earl of Southampton is called "the first heir of his invention," was the first work bearing his name. It was an elegant performance, and served the office, which Bacon doubtless intended it should, of gracefully introducing Shakespeare as a poet to the young wits and poets of London society. Poetry, apart from the drama, was rapidly growing in favor with the young nobility. The exquisite beauty of the poem, the aptness and modesty of the dedication, and the sudden appearance of the rude, untutored player as a poet, must have given an immediate prestige to his name, which was emphasized in a more substantial manner when the first drama bearing it appeared upon the boards of Blackfriars. While by this means the arrangement was assured in its financial aspects, the favorable publicity given to Shakespeare acted as a complete foil to the revealment of Bacon, and Shakespeare was recognized by all as the only author.

It was understood between Bacon and Shakespeare that they "two must be twain," for in their lives there was a "separable spite," which would ever prohibit all social intercourse between them. "I may not," he says in the thirty-sixth Sonnet, "evermore acknowledge thee." A time might come, and that very suddenly, when circumstances would require him to ignore all knowledge of Shakespeare; but whatever might happen to change their relations, they must remain true to each other, and conceal the true origin of the dramas from the world. Shakespeare, as a matter of course, was bound by self-interest, for his fortune was at stake; and Bacon saw nothing but ruin for himself in disclosure. Men thus bound must be true to each other for the protection of their separate interests.

In 1591 Bacon was appointed counsel extraordinary to the queen, an office which obliged his daily attendance upon her majesty. He describes the tediousness of the hours spent in this service in the fifty-seventh and fifty-eighth Sonnets. He must have composed several comedies previous to this time. White thinks that "Love's Labor 's Lost," "The Two Gentlemen of Verona," and the "Comedy of Errors," were written before 1592. It may be fairly inferred, from the continuous history in the poem, that his work upon the dramas suffered no other interruption from this appointment than the hours of service at court. Before 1595, White thinks fourteen of the dramas had been written. How to preserve them, and escape public recognition, was an ever-present cause of fear and annoyance.

In 1594, when Bacon became a candidate for solicitor-general, he bade farewell to play-writing. So confident was he of this appointment, that he determined to abandon it altogether. The separation provided for in his arrangement with Shakespeare was announced in the eighty-seventh Sonnet. In the four or five stanzas succeeding, he declares that the only obstacle to his appointment would be the exposure of his authorship of the dramas. It was a great terror to him, and he was willing to make any personal sacrifice to prevent it. His fears are most vividly portrayed in the ninetieth Sonnet. The hate of Thou and Thy which he there invokes, seemingly to him, furnished his only means of concealment. In the ninety-second Sonnet he writes:—

"I see a better state to me belongs
Than that which on Thy [Thought's] humour doth depend;
Thou [Truth] canst not vex me with inconstant mind,
Since that my life on Thy [Thought's] revolt doth lie."

The seventeen months of suspense, while Bacon and his devoted friend Essex were engaged in the effort to obtain the solicitorship, were full of unhappiness, suspicion, and alarm. At first, as he says in the Sonnets, he found no pleasure even in contemplating the occupation he had abandoned. Soon, however, jealous of what he deemed the failure of other poets, he re-wrote the poem of "Lucrece," which he had composed three years before. This was his only literary work during that period. It was published in 1594, and dedicated to the Earl of Southampton, and as intended, probably, filled the promise of that "graver labor" made in the dedication of "Venus and Adonis."

During this anxious period he spared no efforts to win the solicitorship. He besought his uncle to use his influence with the queen. Not meeting with the encouragement he had a right to expect from him, he attached himself to the young Earl of Essex, who espoused his cause with unremitting energy. In the various electioneering devices resorted to, while the choice was undecided, he, as he says, "made a motley" of himself before the world, "gor'd his own thoughts," and became a beggar for office. The elegant letter, accompanied by a valuable jewel, which he wrote to the queen, attests as well to his eager desire for the appointment as to the measure he had fixed for his own abilities, and the moral dignity and grandeur of his nature. Perhaps his most unfortunate stroke of policy was the one upon which he chiefly relied, that of attaching himself to the Earl of Essex. That young nobleman, though in great favor with Elizabeth, was valued more for his personal accomplishments than his political sagacity. He was also, by reason of the queen's preference, especially obnoxious to Lord Burleigh, and his son, Robert Cecil. Macaulay believes that they connived at Bacon's defeat, and influenced Lord Keeper Puckering to express a preference for some other applicant. It is this opposition of his own kinsmen that Bacon alludes to in the line, "made old offences of affections new." He offended Burleigh and Cecil by his reliance upon Essex.

His confession leaves no room for doubt as to the means he used while in pursuit of the office. His moral delinquences stood as accusing spirits before him. "Most true it is," he writes, "I have look'd on truth askance and strangely." How does this materially differ from the office-seekers of our day? Is there not always in the shifts, turns, and devices, which hope and fear deem necessary to success, a constant warfare upon truth? The ordeal through which he passed during this period is more graphically described in the one hundred and nineteenth Sonnet: —

"What potions have I drunk of Siren tears,
Distill'd from limbecks foul as hell within,
Applying fears to hopes and hopes to fears,
Still losing when I saw myself to win!

> What wretched errors hath my heart committed,
> Whilst it hath thought itself so blessed never!
> How have mine eyes out of their spheres been fitted
> In the distraction of this madding fever."

How many of the great men since Bacon's time, whose experience, like his, was filled with all the sacrifices of principle, honor, and truth, would, as he did, make a full and frank confession of their errors! Yet the name of this great benefactor of our race is almost a synonyme for all that is mean, unscrupulous, and vile in human character. Perhaps the world is not entirely wrong in its denunciations; but if Bacon had concealed his offences as skilfully as he concealed his merits, his memory would stand much fairer in the eyes of posterity. His confessions ruined him. If, as lord chancellor, instead of confessing to a formidable array of acts, all of which had been of customary observance before his time, he had opposed a bold front and insisted upon a trial, there is little doubt that with the king and Buckingham (both of whom it is hinted by Tenison were as blamable as he was) to aid him, he would have escaped that terrible downfall, and that more terrible distich, which in a succeeding age branded him as "the meanest of mankind."

In the fall of 1595 the hopes of Bacon were unexpectedly blasted by the appointment of Sergeant Fleming solicitor-general. The announcement fell upon his ear like a thunderbolt. The disappointment was not so severe as the humiliation. His faith in the influence of Essex with the queen had been from the first an assurance of success. He immediately withdrew from public view, and determined to seek relief for his wounded feelings in travel. The natural buoyancy of his spirits, and the encouragement of Essex, accompanied by a munificent gift, soon dispelled his gloom and sorrow, and he returned to his habits of contemplation and composition. He wrote and published ten essays under his own name, which were greatly admired, and reinstated him in the public favor. He regards them as no substitute in his love for dramatic composition. Alluding to them in the one hundred and tenth Sonnet, he writes to Thee (Thought):—

"And worse *Essays* prov'd Thee my best of love."

The great sorrow he had experienced proved to him his predominant love for closet studies, and especially for dramatic labor. "As easy," he says in the one hundred and ninth Sonnet, "might I from myself depart, as from my soul which in thy breast doth lie."

"For nothing this wide universe I call.
Save Thou, My rose; in it Thou art My all."

In the one hundred and seventh stanza, the death of Queen Elizabeth and the accession of James I. are announced in a single line:—

"The mortal moon hath her eclipse endur'd."

No occurrence at that time could have been more welcome to Bacon. Elizabeth's care for him had always taken the form of a guardian for a ward. She had been no friend to his ambition or his abilities. He follows the announcement of her death with these words:—

> "Incertanties now crown themselves assur'd.
> . . . . . .
> Now with the drops of this most balmy time
> My love looks fresh, and death to me subscribes,
> Since, spite of him, I 'll live in this poor rhyme,
> While he insults o'er dull and speechless tribes."

What were the "incertainties" in Bacon's life which now "crown'd themselves assured"? There is an inner history here alluded to which has never been published,—a history that at the time was not fully revealed, in which Bacon was an actor. Elizabeth always feared that her title to the throne would be disputed, and possibly violently contested by the adherents of Mary Queen of Scots. It was this fear, more than any overt act proved on the trial of the Duke of Norfolk, that caused the death of that unfortunate nobleman. Influenced by this fear, Elizabeth treated Mary as a rival, and when she sought her protection, imprisoned her for eighteen years, tried her for conspiracy, and decapitated her. This same fear, with better cause, led to the death of Essex.

Bacon, by attaching his fortunes to Essex, was defeated by the jealous hostility of Burleigh and Cecil. When, by his unauthorized return from

Ireland, Essex fell under the displeasure of the queen, Bacon, finding it impossible to procure his reinstatement without a trial, prevailed with her majesty to make the inquiry into his conduct extrajudicial in form, and reformatory rather than punitive. The result was a judgment of temporary exile and partial confinement. It was remitted by slow degrees, but the friends of Essex meantime, among their public demonstrations in his favor, caused the play of Henry IV. to be performed for forty nights. One Hayward, a playwright, also read a pamphlet, giving an account of the dethronement of Richard II., which aroused the fears of the queen, who saw in it an attempt to excite the populace to treason. Hayward was arrested and sent to the Tower, and probably saved from a trial that would have cost him his head, by a quick-witted reply of Bacon to the queen's inquiry, "if he could find any places in it that might be drawn in the case of treason." "For treason, madam," he replied, "I surely find none, but for felony, very many." "Wherein?" asked Elizabeth, eagerly. "Madam," said Bacon, "the author hath committed very apparent theft, for he hath taken most of the sentences of Cornelius Tacitus, and translated them into English, and put them into his text."

Bacon always took counsel of his fears. He did not feel safe ever after, while Elizabeth reigned. He wrote nothing except his ten essays and a few tracts until her death. This "incertainty," caused by the performance of his play, — a play commemorative of a usurper, — was, like David's sin, "ever before him." He knew not at what moment it might be revived, or at what moment he might be exposed as its author; but if such moment should come, he knew that his arrest would be certain, and how innocent soever he might have been in purpose, his guilt would be affirmed. Now that Elizabeth was dead, and the Scottish monarch on the throne, this "incertainty" was "assured," his fears vanished, peace reigned, his love looked fresh, and "death" to him "subscribed," or in plainer phrase, surrendered. He was ready to resume work as a dramatist, and as we infer from the one hundred and eleventh and one hundred and twelfth Sonnets, his first drama was "Timon of Athens."

The philosophy which he invoked for Timon was equally applicable to himself. Addressing You (Beauty), he says:—

> "O, for my sake do You with Fortune chide,
> The guilty goddess of my harmful deeds,
> That did not better for my life provide
> Than public means which public manners breeds."

This in effect expressed his intention of writing a drama which should reflect the trial he had passed through. In his own view, it must have been bitter indeed. All his early memories were awakened, when, as the son of one of the first officers of the realm, he was taught to look forward upon a life to be spent in pursuits of his own choice. For this had he been educated, and for this only was he fitted. Fortune decreed otherwise. He had no resource but "public means," and his first effort to improve them by attaining a position had failed. He had made a public exhibition of himself; had been party to many intrigues; had compromised his integrity. Why did not fortune better provide for him? Why was he forced to belie his own great nature and descend to all the tricks, manners, and expenses of an office-seeker? Yet in his case they were unavoidable. He had no other means of livelihood or renown. He continues:—

> "Thence comes it that my name receives a brand,
> And almost thence my nature is subdued
> To what it works in, like the dyer's hand."

The "brand" here alluded to was undoubtedly the aid he gave in the prosecution of Essex. He was charged with ingratitude of the basest kind. Essex had been his devoted friend; aided him in his struggle for position; presented him with a valuable estate; rendered him friendly service in his courtship of Lady Hatton. For these services he had a claim upon Bacon for any assistance he might be able to give. One to read Macaulay's or Campbell's Life of Bacon would conclude that he requited these kindnesses with the blackest ingratitude and inhumanity. Nothing can be farther from the truth. Bacon was the constant friend and adviser of Essex, from the moment that he entered the queen's service until his treasonable attempt to dethrone her. We have already seen that Bacon saved him from a public trial on his ill-advised return from Ireland. It was only after his arrest for high treason that Bacon, unable to assist him further, was obliged, as a loyal subject and counsellor, to aid in his prosecution. Macaulay intimates that he should have refused to act. Campbell thinks that but for his assistance Essex might have escaped. With singular inconsistency both agree that Essex was guilty and deserved his fate. Had Bacon refused his assistance at the trial, he would have been arrested, tried, and punished. Had he failed in the proper discharge of his duties upon the trial, and been detected in attempting to save the earl by diverting the minds of the peers from the testimony, death would have been his certain portion. Essex was arrested in the very act of treason. It was not possible for him to escape conviction. Bacon knew that, having been always an ardent friend and supporter of the earl, all eyes would be turned upon him. The slightest dereliction on his part would be deemed proof of his complicity in the treason. It was impossible for him to aid Essex and save himself. He plainly saw that no aid he could render would alter the result, and that any reluctance on his part to act would be fatal to him.

Who but one that has been placed in a similar situation, and acted differently, has any right to brand Bacon with ingratitude for the course he pursued?

This "brand" upon his name, he intimates, so subdued his nature that he was ready to sacrifice all ambition for advancement, and confine himself to his profession, which, like "the dyer's hand," would take its character from its miscellaneous occupations. It destroyed his confidence in humanity. He describes in the one hundred and twelfth Sonnet the resolution he made for the government of his future life. You (Beauty) have drawn the character of Flavius, the steward of Timon, as a representative of Bacon's disgust at the treatment he received from his professed friends. Among them all, Flavius alone was sincere. The entire stanza, as may be seen by comparing it with the play, is addressed to him. The love and pity which Flavius manifested for Timon in prosperity and adversity; his efforts to save him by warning him of his extravagance; his fruitless expedients to supply means for the payment of his debts; his search for him after he had fled to the woods; the pity he then expressed for him, and the unselfishness of all his acts,—were the "love and pity" that filled the impression which "vulgar scandal" had fastened upon Bacon. That "vulgar scandal" doubtless was his extravagance and impecuniosity, which, as in the case of

Timon, had followed him after his defeat. Unable to pay the debts he had made, deserted by his supposed friends, he wrote this play to commemorate that period of his life, and to signify his distrust of mankind. He delineated his own character,—generous, confiding, humane, liberal in manly features; profuse, improvident, extravagant, and careless in habits. Of these Flavius reminded him, and became thereby "all the world to him." He strove to know "his shames and praises from his tongue," and banished all care, as did Timon, concerning others. All the world beside was dead to him. The philosophy thus invoked for Timon made Bacon a stoic. As his subsequent history proves, he gave himself up to the idea that he would henceforth be indifferent to any judgment the world might form of his acts. He would remain in public life. He was yet young, and in order to rise, he must plead his own merits. This course he ever after pursued. All his letters addressed to James, Buckingham, and Salisbury, seeking promotion, based his claims upon his own special qualifications, often even to the disparagement of others. He was no longer the cringing suppliant of Gray's Inn, but the statesman and confidant of the king. Thus posing as Timon, the charge of ingratitude had no care for him, except perhaps as it might have suggested that great creation of filial ingratitude, King Lear, which was his next drama.

The plays written by Bacon after his defeat took their character from the change which that event had wrought in his life. They were all illustrative of the dark side of human nature. His great tragedies of Lear, Hamlet, Othello, and Macbeth were of this period. His own consciousness of this change, and of its effects upon the dramas, is apparent in the following lines at the close of the one hundred and nineteenth Sonnet:—

"O benefit of ill! now I find true
That better is by evil still made better;
And ruin'd love, when it is built anew,
Grows fairer than at first, more strong, far greater.
So I return rebuk'd to My content,
And gain by ill thrice more than I have spent."

Lear, next in composition to Timon, is very distinctly alluded to in the one hundred and fourteenth and one hundred and fifteenth Sonnets. The marks of identification are unmistakable in the flattery of the old king by his daughters; the reference to the daughters as "monsters" in the resemblance of beauty; the impulsive decrees of Lear, and hastily formed resolution of Gloster, as "things indigest"; the depicture of Goneril, Regan, and Edmund, the perfectly bad as the perfectly best characters of the play, all of which in the next Sonnet are denounced as a lie, in the light of further developments.

The variety and character of Bacon's labors at this time are very astonishing. In public life he was an active member of Parliament, a candidate for knighthood, one of the counsel for the crown on the trial of Sir Walter Raleigh, and an industrious worker for official advancement; while in the closet he was composing tragedies, elaborating his noble treatise on the "Advancement of Learning," planning a "History of England," and preparing a tract for publication on "Helps to the Intellectual Powers."

The Tempest was written at this time. It is fully identified in the one hundred and sixteenth Sonnet. Prospero's love for his brother is foreshadowed in the lines:—

> "Love is not love
> Which alters when it alteration finds."

The remainder of the stanza is suggestive of the other features of the play. He assumes in the next stanza to have written Lear and the Tempest for the purpose of conciliating Beauty, with whom he has been at outs ever since, tempted by the hope of being solicitor, he bade him farewell in the eighty-sixth and eighty-seventh Sonnets. As an apology to him he says, in the one hundred and seventeenth Sonnet:—

> "I did strive to prove
> The *constancy* and *virtue* of your love."

Constancy was the prominent characteristic of Cordelia, and virtue that of Miranda.

Soon after the appearance of Lear and the Tempest, the author, supposed by the writers of the time to be Shakespeare, as it would seem from the one hundred and twenty-first stanza, was charged with plagiarism by some of the play-writers of the time. The reply in the stanza does not deny, but avoids, the charge, and retorts with heavier counter-accusations. Bacon's methods of composition are fully revealed in the poem. Such facts and illustrations as were not of his own conception, he gathered from the works of early authors, classified them under their proper heads of Thought and Beauty, and reproduced them in his own language and imagery as he found occasion. His own thoughts and fancies were jotted down in the same manner, without regard to system or use. One of the most philosophical writers of our day, Ralph Waldo Emerson, is said to have pursued the same method. With the exception of the Tempest and possibly Midsummer Night's Dream, all of Bacon's dramas were founded upon stories of former ages. In the twenty-sixth and fifty-ninth Sonnets these methods are clearly defined. We learn from them that not only for his plots, but for very many of the beautiful thoughts which adorn his dramas, Bacon was indebted to others. He confesses as much in the eighty-seventh Sonnet, when he tells Thy (Thought) that his great gift is growing upon misprision; and in the eighty-eighth, in the words:—

> "With Mine own weakness being best acquainted,
> Upon Thy part I can set down a story
> Of faults conceal'd, wherein I am attainted,
> That Thou in losing me shall win much glory."

The methods so clearly admitted and explained in early life, as the spirit of his reply indicated, disturbed him when they appeared in the form of accusation. Why, he asks, should they, more guilty than he of falsehood and adulteration, "in their wills count bad what he thinks good"? They only expose themselves, and reckon up their own errors. For aught they know, he may be straight. He knows they are not. His deeds must not suffer from their surmises. He was so fearful, however, that they might suffer from this cause, that in the next Sonnet, addressing Thy (Thought), he says that he has committed to memory, for use in Thy's name, where it will remain "above that *idle rank*,"—

"Beyond all date, even to eternity,"—

the "gifts and tables" containing these thoughts; so that they—

"Never can be miss'd.
That poor retention could not so much hold,
Nor need I tallies thy dear love to score;
Therefore to give them from me was I bold,
To trust those tables [memory] that receive thee more:
  To keep an adjunct to remember thee
  Were to import forgetfulness in me."

This "forgetfulness" might betray him, so he destroyed all visible proofs of his methods and his writings. The Promus, a page of his own disconnected thoughts, and a paper indorsed "Ornamenta Rationalia" (Ornaments of Truth), are the only vestiges found among his papers that bear any relation to his dramas.

In the introductory chapter of the Promus, Mrs. Pott says:—

"The Promus was Bacon's shop or storehouse, from which he would draw forth things new and old,—turning, twisting, expanding, modifying, changing them, with that 'nimbleness' of mind, that 'aptness to perceive analogies,' which he notes as being necessary to the inventor of aphorisms, and which, elsewhere, he speaks of decidedly, though modestly, as gifts with which he felt himself specially endowed.

"It was a storehouse of pithy and suggestive sayings, of new, graceful, or quaint terms of expression, of repartee, little bright ideas jotted down as they occurred, and which were made to reappear 'made up,' variegated, intensified, and indefinitely multiplied, as they radiated from that wonderful 'brayne cut with many facets.'"

Mr. Spedding, in his Life of Bacon, after speaking of the miscellaneous character of the collections, says:—

"As we advance, the collection becomes less miscellaneous, as if his memory had been ranging within a smaller circumference. In one place, for instance, we find a cluster of quotations from the Bible, following one another with a regularity which may be best explained by supposing that he had just been reading the Psalms, Proverbs, and Ecclesiastes, and then the Gospels and Epistles (or perhaps some commentary on them), regularly through. The quotations are in Latin, and most of them agree exactly with the Vulgate, but not all. Passing this Scripture series, we again come into a collection of a very miscellaneous character,—proverbs, French, Spanish, Italian, English; sentences out of Erasmus's Adagia; verses from the Epistles, Gospels, Psalms, Proverbs of Solomon; lines from Seneca, Horace, Virgil, Ovid, succeed each other according to some law, which, in the absence of all notes or other indications to mark the connection between the several entries, the particular application of each, or the change from one subject to another, there is no hope of discovering, though in some places several occur together, which may be perceived by those who remember the struggling fortune and uncertain prospects of the writer in those years, together with the great design he was meditating, to be connected by a common sentiment."

At the risk of being thought tedious, and of travelling outside my prescribed field of investigation, I cannot refrain from placing before my readers the carefully expressed opinion formed by Mrs. Pott of the innumerable resemblances she has traced between the Promus and the dramas.

"This is not," she says, "the proper place for discussing the many arguments which have been held for and against the so-called 'Baconian theory' of Shakespeare's plays. Nevertheless, since the publication of these pages is the result of an investigation, the sole object of which was to confirm the growing belief in Bacon's authorship of those plays, and since the comments attached to the notes of the Promus would otherwise have no significance, it seems right to sum up in a few lines the convictions forced upon the mind with ever-increasing strength, as, quitting the broad field of generality, the inquirer pursues the narrow paths of detail and minute coincidence.

"It must be held, then, that no sufficient explanation of the resemblances which have been noted between the writings of Bacon and Shakespeare is afforded by the supposition that these authors may have studied the same sciences, learned the same languages, read the same books, frequented the same sort of society. To satisfy the requirements of such an hypothesis, it will be necessary further to admit that from their scientific studies the two men derived identically the same theories; from their knowledge of languages, the same proverbs, turns of expression, and peculiar use of words; that they preferred and chiefly quoted the same books in the Bible and the same authors; and last, not least, that they derived from their education and surroundings the same tastes and the same antipathies, and from their learning, in whatever way it was acquired, the same opinions and the same subtle thoughts.

"With regard to the natural, and at first sight reasonable, supposition that Bacon and Shakespeare may have 'borrowed' from each other, it would follow that, in such a case, we should have to persuade ourselves, contrary to all evidence, that they held close intercourse, or that they made a specific and critical study of each other's writings, borrowing equally the same kinds of things from each other; so that not only opinions and ideas, but similes, turns of expression, and words which the one introduced (and which perhaps he only used once or twice and then dropped), appeared shortly afterwards in the writings of the other, causing their style to alter definitely, and in the same respects, at the same period of their literary lives. We should almost have to bring ourselves to believe that Bacon took notes for the use of Shakespeare, since in the Promus may be found several hundred notes of which no trace has been discovered in the acknowledged writings of Bacon, or of any contemporary writer but Shakespeare, but which are more or less clearly reproduced in the plays, and sometimes in the Sonnets.

"Such things, it must be owned, pass all ordinary powers of belief; and the comparison of points such as those which have been hinted at impress the mind with a firm conviction that Francis Bacon, and he alone, wrote all the plays and the Sonnets which are attributed to Shakespeare, and that William Shakespeare was merely the able and jovial manager, who, being supported by some of Bacon's rich and gay friends (such as Lord Southampton and Lord Pembroke), furnished the theatre for the due representation of the plays, which were thus produced by Will Shakespeare, and thenceforward called by his name."

The following thoughts, copied almost at random from the 1665 collections comprising Bacon's Promus, with corresponding passages from the plays, will give the reader some idea of his preparatory labors for dramatic composition:—

Silui a bonis et dolor meus renovatus est. — Psalms xxxix.
(I was silent from good words, and my grief was renewed.)

"T is very true my grief lies all within;
And these external manner of laments

Are merely shadows to the unseen grief
That swells *with silence* in the tortured soul."

—*Richard II.*, iv. 1.

Sat patriæ Priamque datum. —*Æneid*, ii. 291.
(Enough has been done for my country and for Priam.)

"Soldiers, this day you have redeem'd your lives,
And show'd how well you love your prince and country."

—*Henry VI.*, 2d pt., iv. 8.

Conscientia mille testes. —*Erasmus's Adagia*, 346; *Quintillian*, v. xi. 41.
(Conscience is worth a thousand witnesses.)

"My conscience hath a thousand several tongues,
And every tongue brings in a several tale,
And every tale condemns me for a villain."

—*Richard III.*, v. 3.

Summum jus summa injuria. —*Cicero Officis*, i. 10.
(The extreme of justice is the extreme of injustice.)

Leontes. "Thou shalt feel our justice in whose easiest passage
Look for no less than death." —*Winter's Tale*, iii. 1.

Dulce et decorum est pro patria mori. —*Horace's Odes*, iii. 2, 13.
(It is sweet and becoming to die for one's country.)

"I'll yield myself to prison willingly,
Or unto death to do my country good."

—*Henry VI.*, 2d pt., ii. 5. See also *Coriolanus*, i. 3; i. 6.

Plumbeo jugulare gladio. —*Erasmus's Adagia*, 490.
(To kill with a leaden sword.)

"You leer upon me, do you? There's an eye
Wounds like a leaden sword."

—*Love's Labor's Lost*, v. 2. See also *Julius Cæsar*, iii. 1.

Haile of Perle. —*Erasmus's Adagia.*

"I'll set thee in a shower of gold,
And hail rich pearls on thee."

—*Antony and Cleopatra*, ii. 5.

Solus currens vincit. —*Erasmus's Adagia*, 304.
(When running alone he conquers.)

"Ye gods, it doth amaze me!
A man of such a feeble temper should
So get the start of the majestic world,
And bear the palm alone." —*Julius Cæsar*, i. 3.

Utilis interdum est ipsis injuria passis. — *Ovid Her.*, xvii. 187.
(Injury is sometimes useful to those who have suffered by it.)

"O sir to wilful men,
The injuries that they themselves procure
Must be their schoolmaster." — *Lear*, ii. 4.

Oleo incendium restiriguere. — *Erasmus's Adagia.*
(To quench fire with oil.)

"Such smiling rogues as these bring oil to fire."
— *Lear*, ii. 2. See also *All's Well*, v. 3; *Merry Wives*, v. 5.

Projicit ampullas et sesquipedalia verba. — *Horace Ars. Poet*, 97.
(Cast aside inflated diction and foot and a half long words.

"They have lived on the alms-basket of words."
— *Love's Labor's Lost*, v. 1.

"Three piled hyperboles, spruce affectation,
Figures pedantical." — *Id.*, v. 2.

Saying and doing two things.

"Your words and your performances are no kin together."
— *Othello*, iv. 2.

Ubi non sis qui fueris non est cur velis vivere.
— *Erasmus's Adagia*, 275.
(When you are no longer what you have been, there is no cause why you should wish to live.)

Shylock. "Nay, take my life and all: pardon not that: —
You take my house when you do take the prop
That doth sustain my house; you take my life
When you do take the means whereby I live."
— *Merchant of Venice*, iv. 2.

"Let me not live, quoth he,
After my flame lacks oil, to be the snuff
Of younger spirits. — *All's Well*, i. 3.

Estimavit divitem omnia jure recta.
(He thought that the rich man was right in all that he did.)

"O, what a world of vile ill-favored faults
Looks handsome in three hundred pounds a year."
— *Merry Wives*, iii. 4.

"Faults that are rich are fair." — *Timon of Athens*, i. 1.

Nolite confidere in principibus. — Psalms cxlvi. 3.
(Put not your trust in princes.)

"O, how wretched is that poor man that hangs on princes' favors,
There is betwixt that smile we would aspire to,
That sweet aspect of princes and their ruin,
More pangs and fears than wars or women have."
Henry VIII., iii. 2.

Collection of sentences by Lord Bacon: —

He that cannot see well, let him go softly.

He that studieth revenge keepeth his wounds green.

Men of noble birth are noted to be envious towards new men when they rise: for the distance is altered; and it is like a deceit of the eye, that when others come on, they think themselves to go back.

In evil, the best condition is, not to will; the next, not to can.

He that goeth into a country before he hath some entrance into the language goeth to school, and not to travel.

In great place ask counsel of both times: of the ancient time, what is best; and of the latter time, what is fittest.

There is a great difference betwixt a cunning man and a wise man; there be that can pack the cards, who yet cannot play well; they are good in canvasses and factions, and yet otherwise mean men.

Extreme self-lovers will set a man's house on fire though it were but to roast their eggs.

You had better take for business a man somewhat absurd than over-formal.

Base natures, if they find themselves once suspected, will never be true.

Men ought to find the difference between saltness and bitterness. Certainly he that hath a satirical vein, as he maketh others afraid of his wit, so he hath need be afraid of others' memory.

Discretion in speech is more than eloquence.

Riches are the baggage of virtue; they cannot be spared, nor left behind, but they hinder the march.

Great riches have sold more men than ever they have bought out.

He that defers his charity till he is dead is, if a man weighs it rightly, rather liberal of another man's than of his own.

Ambition is like choler; if it can move, it makes men active; if it be stopped, it becomes a dust, and makes men melancholy.

To take a soldier without ambition is to pull off his spurs.

A man's nature runs either to herbs or weeds, therefore let him seasonably water the one and destroy the other.

The best part of beauty is that which a picture cannot express.

If you will work on any man, you must either know his nature and fashion, and so lead him; or his ends, and so persuade him; or his weaknesses and disadvantages, and so awe him; or those that have interest in him, and so govern him.

He who builds a fair house upon an ill seat commits himself to prison.

Seneca saith well, that anger is like rain, which breaks itself upon that which it falls.

High treason is not written in ice, that when the body relenteth, the impression should go away.

The best governments are always subject to be like the fairest crystals, wherein every icicle or grain is seen which in a fouler stone is never perceived.

Let states that aim at greatness take heed how their nobility and gentry multiply too fast. In coppice woods, if you leave your staddles too thick, you shall never have clean underwood, but shrubs and bushes.

The master of superstition is the people. And in all superstition, wise men follow fools.

Round dealing is the honor of man's nature; and a mixture of falsehood is like alloy in gold and silver, which may make the metal work the better, but it embaseth it.

It may be fitly remarked here that Bacon's method of composition, of itself, will account for the rare union of Truth, Thought, and Beauty, which has given to all his writings their wonderful predominence over other authors. The whole world of thought, as it had been produced and elaborated by the philosophers, politicians, historians, poets, and polemical writers of former time, had been skimmed by him, and the cream was at his command. This, interwoven with his own thoughts, reproduced in language never equalled before or since, furnishes a rational explanation for the most remarkable features of the dramas. Not alone the poetry, but the wisdom they contained, flowed from this source. They were not the product of a single mind, but as Coleridge truly says, were "myriad-minded." No matter what the passion, what the character, what the power, what the mind to be represented, each in itself reflected what hundreds of philosophers, poets, wits, disputants, orators, had thought and uttered hundreds and thousands of years before. It was the world of life and character in epitome. To wield this vast enginery required the skill and knowledge of a competent engineer. No novice in science or art, no mere genius, however gifted, nothing less than an Olympian mind, fully equipped with learning, philosophy, logic, polemics, imagination, and art, could concentrate, remould, transform, re-create, and replace in living and breathing forms of humanity, this vast assemblage of time-worn, long-forgotten thoughts and truisms. Such an engineer was Francis Bacon. He knew every pulsation, every breath of that complicated machinery, and held it in complete control. It responded to his own impulses, and love, anger, heroism, tyranny, ingratitude, jealousy, ambition, wit, humor, imbecility, and hesitation flowed from it, each in its turn in a form never seen before or attained since.

Referring to the new English Dictionary, now in course of publication, a critic for the Nation says: —

"Every number will be to Shakespearians the cost of the whole book. It will throw a thousand side-lights on Shakespeare's language which they have always longed for, but could never hope to behold. How much of our vocabulary and its significance can be traced back no farther than the great dramatist will be revealed so clearly that he who runs may read. Something of this disclosure may be seen in any fraction of this stupendous work. Turning over the first two hundred pages of the first number, it will be ascertained that one hundred and forty-six words are first found in Shakespeare, either altogether or in some of their meanings. Rome owed only one word to Julius Cæsar. The nature of our debt will be more apparent if we examine some of these hundred and a half of Shakespeare words, all so near the beginning of the alphabet that the last of them is 'air.' We owe the poet the first use of the word 'air' itself in one of its senses as a noun, and in three as a verb or participle. He first said 'air-drawn' and 'airless.'

"Of the one hundred and forty-six words and meanings first given us by Shakespeare, at least two thirds are of classical origin. Baconians will say that such a gift could not by any possibility come from a man of 'small Latin and less Greek.' Others will enlarge their ideas of what Ben Jonson meant by 'small.' The strangest thing seems to be, that so few of Shakespeare's innovations — not so much as one fifth — have become obsolete. He gave them not only life, but immortality. It is perhaps equally noteworthy, that while he was never read so much as to-day, no writer before him (and scarcely one of his contemporaries), cited as authors of words and sentences, is now read at all save by special students."

The next play specially referred to is Cymbéline, in the one hundred and twenty-fourth Sonnet. It is really remarkable that the pointed allusions to the early life of Bacon in this stanza have escaped the notice of all his numerous biographers. He outlines his own history by supposing a similar history for his "own dear love" (his drama), if that were but the "child of state." "It might in that case," he says, "for fortune's bastard be unfather'd." Until the age of twenty, Bacon had not known a want which was not immediately supplied. His genius was recognized by all who knew him. Every possible opportunity, at home and abroad, that colleges, public life, diplomacy, travel, and foreign culture afforded was given to him, and he made a good improvement of them. When he was summoned by the death of his father to return home from France, no young man of that age was more thoroughly accomplished in learning, philosophy, arts, and the elements of statesmanship. Conscious of his own powers, next to a life devoted to speculative and philsophical investigation, of which he saw himself deprived, he was ambitious to fill some public position favorable to his growth in knowledge and usefulness. This was denied him by his uncle and the queen, and being by fortune a "child of state," he was at once as "fortune's bastard unfather'd." In other words, he was a waif at the court of Elizabeth, subject alike to the caprice of the queen and Burleigh's jealousy. His life was wrecked in its spring. No one supplied to him the place of his father. No friend at court took the least interest in the development of his mighty genius. The pictures of his own life suggested to him the character, and doubtless the name, of Posthumus. He, like Bacon, was "unfather'd," and "fortune's bastard," subject, like him, to "Time's love or "Time's hate," both of which he experienced at the hands of Cymbeline and Cloten, as Bacon did at the hands of Elizabeth and Burleigh. He was a "weed among weeds" in his early life, and gathered as a "flower among flowers" afterwards.

This was not the case with his "love" (his drama). That "was builded far from accident" (such as the death of a father). "It suffered not in smiling pomp," as Bacon did in the deceitful smiles of Burleigh and Cecil. Nor did it fall under the blows of "thralled discontent," as both Bacon and Posthumus did in the unkindness of their respective sovereigns. It was not, as those who were heretical at the time, obliged to "work on leases of short-number'd hours," as Bacon was during the nights he devoted to dramatic composition at Gray's Inn. No more faithful picture of the inner life of Bacon can be found in any of his biographies. It leaves us in no doubt as to his own view of the condition in which he found himself placed, and of the impossibility of surmounting it; and it accounts for the sorrowful and piteous letters which he addressed to his uncle and the queen, begging to be relieved, which Macaulay and Campbell have been pleased to cite as evidence of meanness and servility. They could not see under them all the struggles and impatience of a great genius for freedom. They could not realize the crushed and humble spirit of that towering mind, which, as he writes to his uncle, had "as vast contemplative ends as I have moderate civil ends, for I have taken all knowledge to be my province." They could see only "meanness and servility" in that remarkable threat:—

"If your lordship will not carry me on, I will not do as Anaxagoras did, who reduced himself with contemplation unto voluntary poverty; but this I will do, I will sell the inheritance that I have, and purchase some lease of quick revenue, or some office of gain that shall be executed by deputy, and so give over all care of service, and become some sorry book-maker, or a true pioneer in that mine of truth that lies so deep. . . . . I do not think that the ordinary practice of the law, not serving the queen in place, will be admitted for a good account of that poor talent that God hath given me; so as I make reckoning, I shall reap no great benefit to myself in that course."

All the allusions in the one hundredth and twenty-sixth Sonnet point to Hamlet as the next tragedy. Thou (Truth) is addressed as he is illustrated in the tragedy. First, as growing by waning, which is represented by the early experience of Hamlet. He is made to appear as a young scholar called home from college at Wittenberg by the death of his father. His mother soon after is married to his uncle, who thereby succeeds his father as king of Denmark. This hasty marriage, and a vague suspicion that some wrong has been done, preys upon the mind of Hamlet, and he is overcome by grief and misanthropy. He contemplates suicide, and from the first begins to *wane* in his mind, and this waning becomes more and more apparent in his character to the end of the play,—at times putting on a form of qualified derangement. This is undoubtedly what is meant by telling Truth that he has "by waning grown." In the progress, it is shown that the lovers Hamlet and Ophelia became estranged. Their love is finally terminated, and Ophelia is first crazed, then drowned. Thy (Thought) has shown his "lovers' withering," while he is still growing as the tragedy progresses. Nature all this while, who, despite the efforts of Truth and Thought to save the mind and wits of Hamlet, "is the sovereign mistress over wrack," and is gradually unhinging that mind. He is intent upon the vengeance directed by his father's spirit, but as he "goes onward" to inflict it, is still "plucked back," and restrained by doubts, cowardice, and spiritual considerations. Something in his own mind always steps between him and his purpose, to the very end of the play. Nature, meantime, shows "her skill" in disgracing the time, by continuing the guilty love of Claudius and Gertrude, the death of Polonius and Ophelia, the treachery of Rosencrantz and Guildenstern, and the criminal designs of the king upon the life of Hamlet, and thus kills the "wretched moments," which finally end in the violent death of all. She has detained, but not kept, Hamlet, "and her quietus was to render thee," to finally kill him. The motive which instigated Claudius to murder his brother is so fully described in the one hundred and twenty-ninth Sonnet that it needs no interpretation.

Following the narrative, it appears that the successive appearance of the tragedies excited an eager spirit of emulation in contemporary playwrights; and that some of them had chosen their heroes from the colored races. In the one hundred and twenty-seventh stanza he writes: "Now is black beauty's successive heir." These writers had in his opinion failed in their attempts to delineate character truthfully. Beauty was slandered by them, and nature disfigured by art. "Therefore," he says, "My Mistress' brows are raven black," equivalent to saying, "I will see what I can make of a black character." Othello was the product of this determination. This tragedy, as clearly appears from the criticisms he bestowed upon it while in progress, was his most difficult and best approved performance. It was longer time in composition, and the complexion he had chosen for his hero made him doubtful of its success, though he says: "Thy black is fairest in my judgment's place." While engaged in composing it, he contrasted it with the plays of other writers, depicting their ineffectual efforts to imitate him, and the absurdity of their comparisons. His criticisms upon different scenes in the tragedy are alluded to in the one hundred and twenty-seventh, one hundred and thirtieth, one hundred and thirty-first, one hundred and thirty-second, one hundred and thirty-seventh, one hundred and thirty-eighth, one hundred and thirty-ninth, one hundred and fortieth, one hundred and forty-first, one hundred and forty-second, and one hundred and forty-third Sonnets, which are interpreted in the poem.

The choice of a subject for his next tragedy was probably suggested by a desire to please King James. It was Macbeth, the first and only drama for which the subject was chosen from Scottish history. He had glorified England by a reproduction of the "War of the Roses." Some of his best productions were located in Italy. Denmark and Bohemia had been honored each with a drama, but the Scotch were entirely neglected. While Elizabeth lived it would have been imprudent to introduce a play of Scottish origin, as her fears all came from that quarter, but nothing could be more acceptable to James. The time, not less than the subject, was well chosen. The union between Scotland, Ireland and England, so long the cause of unhappy differences between those countries, had been happily effected by the succession of

James. He had been four years on the English throne when the tragedy appeared. A flattering allusion was made to the union by a symbol seen by Macbeth in some of the kings of "Banquo's time," which passed in vision before him on his visit to the witches,—

> "And some I see,
> That twofold balls, and trebled sceptres carry."

A belief in witchcraft pervaded all classes at this time. King James in 1597 had published a work on Demonologie, at Edinburgh, which after his succession to Elizabeth, was reprinted in London. In the preface he reminds the reader of the "fearful abounding in this country of these detestable slaves of the devil, the witches or enchanters." The writer of Macbeth had no faith in the infallibility of witchcraft. It is not improbable that he intended by this tragedy to indirectly compliment King James's book, by depicting the terrible consequences of a reliance upon the fortune-telling jugglers of this period. No moral essay on the subject could have more fearfully predicted them than this great tragedy. A law had been passed during the first year of the reign of James on the English throne, punishing witchcraft in all its forms with death. In the Sonnet, as in the drama, Bacon treats it as a delusion, but makes Macbeth obey it as a divine command. "Buy terms divine in selling hours of dross," is the last of all the fugitive consolations he recommends to Macbeth, when his castle is besieged, and his capture and death assured. His own idea of fortune-telling and astrology is very plainly described in the fourteenth Sonnet.

Next to Macbeth, as appears from the Sonnets, Bacon composed Antony and Cleopatra. This was his last dramatic labor. This tragedy was probably completed in 1607, — the year that Bacon received the appointment of solicitor-general. We are thus brought to the close of this remarkable allegorical history of his career as the writer of the plays attributed to Shakespeare. Let us briefly summarize what it has taught us:—

1. It contains a cipher, or key of words, — very simple, easy of comprehension, and unfailing through all the stanzas from the first to the last. It is impossible to resist the idea that Thou means Truth; Thy, Thought; and You, Beauty. These are the three allegorical characters whose aid Bacon constantly invokes in the creation of the impersonation he calls "My Love," which answers completely to the title, "My Drama," or "My Dramas." The impersonation "My Friend" is only used on two occasions, — twice in the forty-second Sonnet, to signify the transfer of "My Love" to him, and three times in the one hundred and thirty-second Sonnet, where ownership and authorship are abandoned and made over to him. "My Mistress" appears in the one hundred and twenty-seventh stanza as descriptive

of Othello, and is described in the light of false comparison in the one hundred and thirtieth, and as the only spring which will cure his love in the one hundred and fifty-third and one hundred and fifty-fourth; but her character adapts itself to all the tragedies that he wrote, and by allusion and allegory, appears as if a part of each one. Hence she answers to the name of Tragedy. All other ciphers are single, and easily understood. The entire poem is so perfectly sustained in its allegorical illustration and expression that it forms one grand cipher; every form of metaphor and metonymy, the loftiest imagination, the subtlest induction, the profoundest philosophy, are used to conceal, and yet contain, the great secret of the authorship of the dramas attributed to Shakespeare. The poem, for the purposes intended by the author, is a masterpiece, without a rival or an imitation in English literature.

2. From the first to the eighteenth Sonnets, in the reasons addressed to Thou, Thy, and You, as the respective representatives of Truth, Thought, and Beauty, and to the gifts of nature (all of which he claims as parts of himself), we learn why he was induced to engage in the illustration of life in character. He reasons with himself through the medium of each separate element of his genius, and treating each as a laggard, persuades all to engage in the production of some great labor, which shall win for him an immortal name.

3. From the eighteenth to the eighty-seventh, the period of his first labors as an author are described. He is satisfied that his work will live. His outcast state, disappointments, and sorrows are depicted in contrast with the delight he experiences in writing. His methods of composition, and hours devoted to it, the places where he writes, his careful concealment of his tables and manuscripts, his discontent during his hours of enforced absence, are described. The nature of his arrangement with Shakespeare, the interest he has in the avails flowing from it, the relationship they are to bear to each other, his delight on seeing the dramas in theatrical representation, his opinion of imitators and contemporary playwrights, his daily attendance upon Queen Elizabeth, are all distinctly set forth. He tells his name; alludes to the work he contemplates doing in philosophy; describes the enigmatical dedication of the Sonnets; announces his intention soon to abandon writing for a public position; alludes to a rival poet; sees his own lines in another's work.

4. From eighty-seventh to one hundred and seventh: he bids farewell to dramatic composition, to engage in an effort to obtain a public position. His fears lest he should be discovered as a playwright are fully portrayed in the eighty-eighth, eighty-ninth, and ninetieth stanzas. He invokes his own powers and Shakespeare in the strongest terms not to betray him; he is tortured with *en-*

nui, and finds fault with the poetry of his contemporaries; tells wherein it is unnatural; calls upon his Muse to resume labor; rewrites the poem of "Lucrece," which was composed three years before; compares it favorably with other poems.

5. From one hundred and seventh to one hundred and fifty-fourth: he intimates the defeat of his hopes in the one hundred and nineteenth Sonnet, and his delight at being able to re-engage in dramatic composition; his dramas look fresh; neither his fears that he might be betrayed, nor the prophecy that he would be elected, now that he is defeated, can prevent his return to his love; Queen Elizabeth is dead, and James I. is king; his prospects are improved; the times are better; he confesses his errors; refers to his essays, preferring his dramas; depicts his disappointments, and his determination in future, in the tragedy of Timon; follows Timon with Lear, and Lear with the Tempest; resents the charge of plagiarism; destroys his collections of thoughtful sayings, and the tables on which his own thoughts are written; writes Cymbeline; depicts his own life in the character of Posthumus; writes Hamlet; follows it with Othello, which he criticises closely, and pronounces it his best tragedy; ridicules the writers who attempt to imitate him; abandons the authorship and property of the dramas to Shakespeare, and devises methods for his own concealment; writes Macbeth, which is followed by Antony and Cleopatra, his

last dramatic production; names his Mistress (Tragedy) as the only cure for his love.

Anticipating that the time would soon arrive, when, by a change in his position, and perhaps a desire to devote his leisure to his great philosophical treatise, the Novum Organum (already in progress), Bacon, as appears in the one hundred and thirty-third, one hundred and thirty-fourth, one hundred and thirty-fifth, and one hundred and thirty-sixth Sonnets, abandoned all his interest in the dramas in favor of Shakespeare, under the strongest injunctions of secrecy. That he regretted this sacrifice is everywhere apparent in the Sonnets; but he could see no other method of avoiding discovery, and attaining to the public honors now almost within his grasp. Thenceforward his rise in public life was rapid. He held the office of solicitor-general until 1613. He was then appointed attorney-general, which office he held until his elevation to the lord chancellorship in 1617. In 1621 he was tried and found guilty of bribery by his peers, expelled from his office, sentenced to pay a fine of forty thousand pounds, imprisoned in the tower, and declared "incapable of holding any office of trust, honor, or employment." The king pardoned him. He was released from imprisonment in a day or two, the fine was remitted, and before his death all the disabilities of his sentence were removed. Unbroken in spirit, he continued through all these changes to pursue his philosophical investigations with unflagging zeal and energy. The great works bearing his name are the result of these labors. He died in 1626.

In 1623, seven years after the death of Shakespeare, the dramas in revised form were published in a folio under the apparent superintendence of Hemings and Condell, two former associates of Shakespeare. Many changes were made in the plays by addition and suppression, which were claimed to be corrections from original copies. No suspicion of the authorship existing, they escaped public scrutiny at the time, and have been received by all ages since, until the present, as the undoubted works of William Shakespeare. Those of our readers who receive as true the interpretation herein given of the Sonnets will have no doubt that the folio was published under the careful supervision of Lord Bacon, and that all the changes, emendations, suppressions, and additions were made by him. Those who believe or think differently cannot be convinced without more positive evidence. We leave the subject there.

WILLIAM SHAKESPEARE.

Conjecture, tradition, and fable have been busy for the past two hundred and seventy years in fabricating a life for William Shakespeare. Relieved of those three elements, the facts in that life could be told on a single page of foolscap. It would contain nothing suggestive of uncommon genius or ability. By adding to the grains of truth found in the biographies of commentators such facts as are disclosed in the Sonnets, we learn that he was a wild, uncultivated young man in Stratford, clever in his own conceit, full of life and frolic, ready to join in any boyish mischief, and careless of its results. He was no worse than nine tenths of the young men who permit themselves to be swayed by passion and a love of notoriety. Whatever the motive that induced him to go to London, certain it is, that on his arrival there, he abandoned his reckless habits and addressed himself to business. How he became acquainted with Lord Bacon, or why he was selected to father his dramas, we leave to conjecture. Some peculiarity of his life prompted Bacon to make an arrangement with him by means whereof his plays were represented in the theatre, Shakespeare recognized as their author, and Bacon a joint sharer in the avails they produced.

As we read the character of Shakespeare in the Sonnets, he was entirely uncultivated, but true, honest, faithful, and thrifty, and at the time he became known to Bacon, a share-holder in Blackfriars Theatre, and a general favorite among his fellow-actors and play-writers. He was also sufficiently familiar with managerial methods to adapt the plays to the stage, and was intrusted with that service by Bacon. He kept his promise to Bacon of entire secrecy from the moment of their acqaintance in 1590, and died with it undivulged in 1616. The dramas were written during the first twenty years of that period. Shakespeare, meantime, acquired a handsome property, and soon after Bacon ceased to write in 1609, retired to his native village to enjoy it.

Very little is known about the closing years of his life. He was careful of his estate, and a successful business man. Divested of the falsities with which a veneration for his supposed writings have endowed his memory, and viewed only as a plain man of the world, there is nothing reproachful in the lawful methods he employed to collect the debts justly owing to him, nor is it very strange or criminal that he should have purchased his family memorials at the Herald's office. The

Sonnets give him the credit of being kind and just, and his contemporary playwrights all express the highest respect for his memory. Bacon exonerates him from all original design in the plan and arrangement by which he became known as the author of the plays, and takes the blame entirely to himself.

The cause of his death, usually assigned, rests upon tradition, and may or may not be true. There is nothing very remarkable about it. He had been an actor and stage manager. His life had been passed among convival companions, who drank, sang, and had their hours of mirth and hilarity. If his excesses, while enjoying a visit from Jonson and Drayton, produced a fever of which he died, it is quite as reasonable, and much more charitable, to infer that it was the effect of violence to his abstemiousness rather than to his inordinate love of liquor. Whatever the cause, he died at the age of fifty-one, in April, 1616, and was buried in Stratford church, where, protected by the objurgatory lines on his tomb, his body doubtless long ago crumbled back to its mother earth.

There is nothing in the history revealed in the Sonnets which requires a more elaborate biography of Shakespeare. None of the numerous traditions, conjectures, and fables which have been accepted as events by commentators and critics during the past 270 years are of the least importance, unless he was the true author of the works bearing his name. With that established as a fact, they are invaluable; because everything relating to him would then be invaluable. In a discussion of his claims to the authorship of the dramas, they serve only to mislead and bewilder, while they prove nothing but the devotion and energy of those who wrote them. Shakespeare's memory has been defamed and exalted by them. The same writers who assign to him the foremost place in literature give him an infamous personal character. If the Sonnets are true as herein interpreted, both these conclusions are false, and William Shakespeare, averaged with the men of his age, was better than the most of them.

ADDENDA.

Several passages in the Sonnets would seem to indicate that Bacon chose Shakespeare as his representative because of his capacity for money getting and his literary deficiencies. Shakespeare was a share-holder in Blackfriars Theatre in three years after he came to London. He could be safely trusted as a financier. Ignorant in a literary sense, and unconscious of any ability as a writer, he indulged no higher ambition than to achieve a competency and return to Stratford. Critics and commentators all regard his utter indifference to the dramas, and his inordinate love of money, as the most unaccountable features of his character. They treat those defects pathetically, and offer apologies for them which would be scorned if offered in behalf of any man but Shakespeare.

Money and ignorance were what Bacon needed in a representative. The first was a necessity of his life; the last of his safety. Both were assured in Shakespeare. He could not have trusted the dramas to men of culture like Ben Jonson, Peele,

Marlow, or Green, for fear of interpolations or suggestions. Shakespeare saw nothing in them for himself but money. The fame never entered his mind. If it did, he abandoned it for the wealth he could not otherwise have acquired. It was through that ignorance and indifference that they were preserved in the form in which they were written.

The remarkable passage in Bacon's will leaving "his name and memory to men's charitable speeches, to foreign nations, and to the next ages," and the equally remarkable lines on Shakespeare's tomb forbidding the removal of his remains, are enigmas in the history of each which no commentator has been able to solve. Why should either of them have been written? If there was nothing more to revere Bacon for than the great works which bore his name, which name, when he died, was more revered than any other in the world of letters, what was there for "foreign nations or the next ages" to do which would add to his fame? They could not wipe away his stains, nor add to his renown. Both were history. But if they should discover that to his philosophical works the great dramas must be added, they would receive that great "name and memory" as the grandest bequest ever bestowed by man upon his race; they would be charitable to his errors and exalt his fame in all nations.

So of Shakespeare, who died the recognized and

accepted author of the dramas. Why should he have a curse upon his tomb for any one who ventured to remove his remains to Westminster Abbey? Was not this also attributable to the calm foresight of Bacon? He saw that a time would come, in his own or a foreign land, when the world would know and acknowledge him as the author of the dramas. He knew that when that occurred, if Shakespeare's remains had been removed to Westminster Abbey, it would be regarded as an impious profanity, by both him and Shakespeare, of the great national mausoleum of England's worthies, and blacken his name and memory forever. He determined that neither should repose there. Hence the pathetic reason given in his will for requesting that his own burial should be in St. Michael's Church, within the limits of Old Verulam. "There," he says, "was my mother buried."

It is a curious fact in the lives of both Bacon and Shakespeare, that no avowed knowledge of each other appears in their authenticated works. How could it be possible for two such men to dwell in the same city twenty-six years, and be engaged in writing on cognate subjects, without some sort of mutual recognition? Difference in social life might prove an obstacle to personal acquaintance, but could it, by any possibility, make them strangers to each other's writings? Would those grand creations of Hamlet, Othello, Macbeth, and Timon escape the philosophical acumen of so keen an observer of life and manners as Bacon? Would not Shakespeare, with his love of nature and truth, have sought and found more than appears in his imputed works, in the Essays and De Augmentis, to enrich his soliloquies? Yet neither mentions the name of the other, or quotes a single passage from his works. One would not know from the works of the other that he had ever lived, yet each in his line was the most remarkable man of that remarkable age. Neither failed of admirers in his contemporaries, but of Shakespeare it may be truly said, that, aside from the dedications of "Venus and Adonis" and "Lucrece," he never bestowed a word of praise or blame upon any one. Bacon loved the drama, treated of it philosophically, and it is believed by many, contemplated in one part of the Novum Organum to employ it in the illustration of life in character. He was on terms of social intimacy with Ben Jonson, who often acted as his amanuensis, and under his direction translated many of his works into Latin. Did Bacon and Shakespeare slight each other? or was it pure oversight that each escaped the other's notice?

It would be surprising that the key to this poem had not been discovered two centuries ago if Bacon was at that time suspected of its authorship. That he was not renders the discovery all the more interesting and valuable now, as it gives an intelligible meaning to those allegorical passages which have so long stained the memory of Shakespeare. Whatever the errors of Bacon, his private character was irreproachable. He had no adventures to tell, no impurities to confess. His life was divided between his public duties and his closet studies. With the key to unlock his meaning, it is not necessary to expose the gallantries and irregularities of any of the young noblemen of Elizabeth's court to find one whom "Thou," in all his tergiversations will fit. The simple word "Truth" answers to every charge, and makes a plain narrative of that which in any other view is inexplicable. Neither is it necessary to reveal the frailties of any of the noble ladies of that day to find a counterpart for "You" and "My Love," when Beauty is so clearly signified by one and "My dramas" by the other. Nor is there any need that poor Will Shakespeare, a man doubtless not without faults like other men, should confess to an indulgence and excess of passion so infamously mean, that the great memory he bears scarcely saves him from universal execration. "My Love," "Thy," and "My Friend" are the only terms by which he can be recognized in the poem. Then there is "My Mistress," that black, diabolical woman of whom it is written,—

> "For I have sworn thee fair and thought thee bright,
> Who art as black as hell, as dark as night."

When you call her Tragedy, all the mystery which

enshrouds her life disappears, and the story in allegory is fully revealed. The symbols, comparisons, metaphors, correspondences, and allusions become instinct with meaning. Events are told as they occur, experiences as they are realized. Disappointments are explained, and sorrows faithfully depicted, and all are conformable to the life and character of Bacon, whose name appears as a guaranty of their truth. There are but four persons who ever lived alluded to in the poem: Bacon, Shakespeare, Queen Elizabeth, and another poet; all the others are allegorical. What more?

www.ingramcontent.com/pod-product-compliance
Lightning Source LLC
Chambersburg PA
CBHW020502270326
41926CB00008B/710

* 9 7 8 3 3 3 7 0 6 3 1 3 9 *